# 2017
# THE BEST MEN'S
# STAGE MONOLOGUES

2017
The Best Men's
Stage Monologues

# 2017
# THE BEST MEN'S
# STAGE MONOLOGUES

## Edited and with a Foreword
## by Lawrence Harbison

### MONOLOGUE AUDITION SERIES

SMITH AND KRAUS PUBLISHERS                    2017

ISBN: 9781575259147
Library of Congress Control Number: 2329-2709


Typesetting and layout by Elizabeth E. Monteleone
Cover by Olivia Monteleone




A Smith and Kraus book
177 Lyme Road, Hanover, NH 03755
editorial 603.643.6431 To Order 1.877.668.8680
www.smithandkraus.com

# Table of Contents

# FOREWORD

Here you will find a rich and varied selection of monologues for men, most of which from plays which were produced and/or published in the 2016-2017 theatrical season. Many are for younger performers (teens through thirties) but there are also some excellent pieces for older men as well. The age of the character is indicated in each monologue, but you will find that many may be done by actors of different ages. Some are comic (laughs), some are dramatic (generally, no laughs). Some are rather short, some are rather long. All represent the best in contemporary playwriting.

Several of the monologues are by playwrights whose work may be familiar to you, such as Don Nigro, Theresa Rebeck, Steven Dietz, Sheila Callaghan, Aaron Posner, Yussef El Guindi, Jacquelyn Goldfinger, Alexandra Gersten-Vassilaros and Halley Feiffer; others are by exciting up-and-comers such as Nicole Pandolfo, Graham Techler, Gregory Strasser, Kim Davies, Ana Nogueira, Alana Valentine, Carey Crim and Mashuq Mushtaq Deen.

Many of the plays from which these monologues have been culled have been published and, hence, are readily available either from the publisher/licensor or from a theatrical book store such as The Drama Book Shop in New York. Some may not be published for a while, in which case contact the author or his agent to request a copy of the entire text of the play which contains the monologue which suits your fancy. Information on publishers/rights holders may be found in the Rights & Permissions section in the back of this anthology.

NOTE: the monologue copy indicates age, race and sex of the character as originally conceived by the playwright. Many monologues could be used in class or for auditions by any age, race or sex.

Break a leg in that audition! Knock 'em dead in class!

Lawrence Harbison

*The Monologues*

# ALIVE AND WELL

## Kenny Finkle

Seriocomic
Carla, thirties

*Carla, a writer, is speaking to Zach, a Civil War nut. She thought she was being paid by a magazine to write about a mysterious ghost known as the "Lonesome Soldier;" but has just found out that it was Zach who hired her, and that there is no Lonesome Soldier. She has torn up his second payment. He has apologized to her for misleading her.*

### CARLA

It takes great bravery to do something despite its foolishness. And passion. It takes great passion. And I respect that, more than respect it, I – desire it. I want to live my life like you live your life. Well, not literally, because from all I've seen, your life is clearly a mess but your passion…Mr.Clemenson, your passion is something to be envied. I feel terrible about the cashier's check Mr. Clemenson. That was a lot of money to have raised and I should not have destroyed it so cavalierly. That was…wrong of me. And because I have no way of paying the money back, I believe the only correct thing to do is to continue with my professional duties. And because I insist on us remaining professional there will be no more personal outbursts where one of us says something like "you're a 100% bonafide real deal not farb in the least authentic knockout" or whatever it was you said. You hired me to do a job and this job is not complete. I will write your story for you and you will be able to do whatever you want with it – try to sell it to a magazine, put it on the internet, whatever you desire. We will go to Appomattox. You wanted me to see it and I want to see it now that you've explained to me why it is so important to you. We are going to go on foot because that's how you wanted us to go. And we're way off course, which means we have a lot of walking to do but we're going to do it and we're going to make it there by April 9th, because that was your plan. And we're going to follow your plan and do this. Do you understand me?

# ALIVE AND WELL

*Kenny Finkle*

Seroconic
Zach, thirties

*Zach, a Civil War nut, has agreed to go along with a writer, who has been hired by a magazine (she thinks) to write about a Confederate ghost known as the "Lonesome Soldier." Turns out, it is Zach who has paid her.*

## ZACH

The Lonesome Soldier. I'm the Lonesome soldier, ok? You got me. I surrender. Actually there are three of us. I got a couple of buddies – we trade off playing the Lonesome Soldier, one of 'em was supposed to show up for us sometime yesterday, another one on the first day but I suppose we missed them on account of the faulty compass and then the rain. We had some pretty spooky stuff planned but none of it worked out. At least not in the way I planned it. At first the Lonesome Soldier was gonna antagonize you for being a Yankee, he was gonna try to make you feel what it was like to be in the war. And then he was gonna try to explain his side of things, tell you about everything that led up to the surrender, what it meant to surrender, how it felt, so that when you got to Appomattox you'd really understand it, you'd really feel it. And Ms. Keenan, Appomattox! Appomattox is just something to behold! And to think of what happened there! To stand there and know it happened right there, well that's just – that's just – I knew if nothing else that Appomattox would make you see! And you'd be able to write the story that was supposed to be told and people would want to come down here and see and hear it all for themselves. And if that worked, I'd have fulfilled something for myself. I would have achieved something great. I believe so much in this story Ms. Keenan. I believe that there's something for all of us to learn from the story of the surrender, from what happened at Appomattox, something that we all need in our lives. I believe if people really could understand that story that our country could change, could get better. And if I could do that, my life could have meaning. And I want my life to mean something. I shouldn't have done any of this. I see that now. But I couldn't help it. Regina, she kept telling me this was stupid. She thinks I'm a fool. Thinks that everything I believe in is foolish, a waste of time.

She thinks I should go work a regular job. That's what she says. Go get a regular job and give up this dream. But I couldn't help it, it's my passion. You know what I mean, don't you? You have a passion too. You know what it means to have a passion. Don't you? I know you do. Last night when you were talking about your grandmother and her work, her art, I saw it in you. I saw your passion. And I don't care if it was the whiskey that was talking, I liked that whiskey tinged Carla Keenan last night and when you were up and singing that song I looked at you and something opened up in me and I feel kind of ridiculous saying it right now but for the record I gotta tell you - Ms. Keenan I think you're a 100% bonafide real deal not farb in the least authentic knockout. Do you hate me? I don't blame you if you do. Do you? You do. It's ok. I hate myself.

# ALIVE AND WELL
## Kenny Finkle

Dramatic
Zach, thirties

*Zach, a Civil War nut, has been travelling with a writer named Carla, who thinks she has been hired by a magazine to write a story about a mysterious Confederate ghost, but she has found out that, in fact, it was Zach who hired her. By the end of the play, though, she's hooked on the Civil War, and the two of them have come to Appomattox, where Zach sets the scene of Lee's surrender. This speech couldn't be more timely.*

### ZACH

Alright, so all through the night of April 8th and into the early morning of April 9th, the two Generals send letters back and forth and finally they agree to meet right here. Lee arrives first and waits. Grant comes soon thereafter and for a period of several minutes the two men are by themselves. After four long years of war, hundreds of thousands of men killed, land, property, towns, cities destroyed, it all comes down to these heroes, Generals of opposing Armies, these two men, just flesh and blood, deciding the fate of our country. That's a scene I'd love to re-enact. That's delicate stuff right there. Because it's not just about the surrender. It's about what happens after the surrender. Most countries split apart for good after a Civil War. But we didn't. We did something very different and it's all because of these two men who found a way to really see and hear each other. I'd like to think I could do that, but I don't know if I could. That's something to strive for I think. Something to be better at. The seeing and the hearing of each other. The ability in the most difficult moment to look ahead with hope, accept the tensions between us and choose for a greater good to unite.

Lawrence Harbison

# ALLIGATOR

## *Hillary Bettis*

Seriocomic
Ty, nineteen

*Ty and his twin sister Emerald are alligator wrestlers. The show is about to begin. This is his pitch to the spectators.*

### TY

Weeeeelcome, weeeeelcome, weeeeelcome ya'll from all over the country! All over the world! All over the universe! All over where ever the hell it is ya'll are from! Now I hope ya'll are ready to be amazed here today. Are ya ready? I said are ya ready? Oh now folks, I can't hear ya! Now I wanna hear ya loud as a pig in a slaughterhouse! Loud as a pig squealin' for his life! That means you gotta scream loud as ya can! You gotta scream so loud every single 'gator in the swamp over there can hear ya! Are ya ready?

*(He gestures.)*

Louder!

*(He gestures until the tourists respond.)*

Wonderful! Wonderful! Now I'm Ty and this here is my twin sister, Emerald. I wrestle the deadliest, scariest, most dangerous 'gators in all of the Everglades! I wrestle 'gators that make all the other 'gators in the swamp shiver to the bone with fear! I wrestle 'gators that are so gigantic they don't even exist in a Hollywood movie! An Emerald over here has this uncanny ability to peer into the deepest, darkest realms of the 'gators' mind! Ya hear that? She can read minds, folks! She knows what ya'll are thinkin' right now! Ooooooh! Scary! Better stop thinkin' them evil thoughts guy in the blue shirt. I'm just foolin'. She don't read human minds. Now folks, now I just wanna prepare ya for what ya'll are gonna witness here, OK? Anything, an I mean ANYTHING at any moment could go wrong! There could be blood! There could be buckets of blood! An we'd be piss outta luck 'cause we don't got health insurance! I sure hope there's a doctor out there who can sew an arm back on... for free! Now folks, now here's the clincher all right? Me an Em are just poor orphan children, livin' alone in the swamps... Just tryin' to make it one day at a time... Our parents, God rest their souls, died in a bloody car crash an left us behind ta pay their gamblin' debt. It's a real tragedy, folks. Somedays we can't even afford ramen noodles... Now, at the end of our show, if ya'll aren't completely blown away by our unique abilities, ya don't gotta pay the admission fee! But just remember that we're just orphans an we might starve ta death if ya don't, folks! An feel free ta throw a tip in there if ya like.

Lawrence Harbison

# AMAZING

## *Brooke Berman*

Dramatic
Nicky, eighteen

*Nicky and her more confident best friend Isobel (eighteen) are making a cinema-verite style documentary about themselves the summer after freshman year. When Isobel invites Nicky to move in, Nicky plays it cool but then, tells the camera just how much she wants to stay. Note: Both Isobel and Nicky have moms named Carla.*

### NICKY

The thing is, it's like this. My mom, who has the same name as yours, she's home with her husband, that guy who isn't my dad, and they don't get along too well, and neither one of them gets along with me, and it's better if I'm not there at all because things move there, things move and break—our dishes, glassware, furniture and bodies—things have a way of finding themselves on the other side of the room, they get thrown and they fly, and I get in the way. I don't have any bruises to prove how I get in the way, but I do - get in the way. The dishes hit the wall, and I get called names - "Selfish bitch" and "stupid little slut" - which is wildly funny since I'm an eighteen year old virgin with kickass SAT scores and nothing like a stupid slut, whatever he thinks that means - but it's better than what he calls my mom. And what she calls him back. Because let's note that my mom is not a victim of this name-calling mean garbage, she's a full-on participant. It is a mutual game of torture. Search and destroy. Carla and That Guy search, and they destroy. Each other. And then me. So I love the idea of not going home. I totally love it. Hugely. Deeply. I'm all over it. Yes. I can stay.

*Brooke Berman*

Dramatic
Tiger, eighteen

*Tiger has been locked away at rehab all year. On the eve of coming home,
he writes a provocative email to his ex-girlfriend Isobel.*

### TIGER

Hola Compadres. Hi there. Hey. Subject line: Coming Home, Home-
coming, not a deliberate reference to that dance. Heinous custom, that
dance. So yeah. Hola. Hey. Dear Friends at Home. I'm getting out
of here in a few weeks. Coming back. Want to hang out? I've been
thinking about you and I want to hang out again like we used when
we used to do that. You know? how we used to get Italian lemonade
(cuz I am not allowed to drink beer and smoke pot), sit in your hall-
way, sit around outside the library and watch people? I'm really sorry
about the way I took all of you for granted, used your houses as crash
pads when my Dad threw me out, made you hold my stash, passed
out, hid out, threw up, all that - and about all those times I just, you
know, "stole" if that's what you want to call it. But – hey—Isobel.
Dear Isobel, dear razorsedge@hotmail, I've been thinking about the
way we used to stay up late and look at the stars and call each other
when it rained. Been thinking about that thing you said when we were
going out. You said I'd never be lost again. You said I would never be
lost because you have an internal compass and I would have you. But
I don't have you anymore and I just want to know, were you lying?
When you said that? Were you lying?

*He puts the pen down.*

Fuck it. I'll just show up.

# AMAZING

## Brooke Berman

Dramatic
Rexx, nineteen to twenty-one

*Isobel (eighteen) and Nicky (eighteen) are making a cinema-verite style documentary about themselves the summer after their freshman year of college. When they meet new friend Rexx, at the coffee shop where he and Nicky both work, it's only natural that they'd invite him to move in with them and collaborate on the film. Here, Rexx describes "home" to the camera.*

### REXX

Home is a good place. I like it at home. I left, but I like it. My mom's downstate. She has eight kids. She lives in that community. My dad lives somewhere else. He wasn't into the whole community thing, I guess. He's pretty straight-laced. So, home's okay, I guess. Couldn't wait to leave, but I guess it's okay. Here, in Chicago, I live with boys. The House of Boys, we call it The House of Boys because only boys live there. I know them from the restaurant. We all worked together at the restaurant. Here was the fun thing about the restaurant—pretending the cappuccino maker was broken. (I'm sorry, Sir, you can't have a cappuccino; the machine's broken." Big Smile for Tip.) Here was the bad thing: uh… everything else. But I'm gonna have a home someday. Home is the place where you can just be who you are. Where you don't pretend. Where you don't have to be perfect or quiet or take care of anyone you don't want to. Where you can be "at home". Nicky says that sometimes that takes a while to figure out.

# THE ARSONISTS

*Jacqueline Goldfinger*

Dramatic
H, fifties

*M and H were a father-daughter arson team. A fire they set went awry, he died, but she is holding onto his ghost. He is trying to convince her to let him go, find peace in the hereafter, and that she's got to understand that she can't control everything no matter how good she is or thinks that she is.*

### H

You'd like tigers, Littles. Tigers always in flames. Stripes shimmer, Just with the walkin' of it. An' when it runs, Shit, Looks like fire spreadin' through the trees. From soil to sky, tall pines, row on row on row, with this streak of fire runnin' through it, leavin' nothin' behind. No smoke. No ashes. The cleanest burn you ever seen. A tiger's the best controlled burn. You'd be jealous ah that Littles. Even you with a hun'red packs ah matches couldn't do that. Burn so clean you leave nothin' behind. An' there he be. On fire standin' still. You can't be a tiger, all heat an' power an' control. You can't control the fire that good. Neither can I. Whether it be the fire or the heat or the police or the sheer weight of time There's always somethin' more than you, Littles. Somethin' out of your control … The wind kicks It kicks at the moment I light the head fuse. It catches my hand and wrist collar. Jump cross my arms, melts the buttons from my … At, when, at that, when it jumped, cross my body. That's when I knew it. And I look across the field at you, Just doin', what I taught you, Just, shinin' in our own light. I knew you's ready. And I knew I's done. I said goodbye to you then, Littles. You couldn't get 'cross that field in-time unless you flew. And that's one I couldn't teach. What you can do now, Put me in the ground, give me peace. Leave. Start somethin' new. You can control that. You got a tiger by the tail, Doodlebug. You think you own it now, but that's a trick. It already owns you. You don't get out, it'll take what it wants in the end.

For information on this author,
click on the WRITERS tab at www.smithandkraus.com.

# THE ARSONISTS

*Jacqueline Goldfinger*

Dramatic
H, fifties

*M and H were a father-daughter arson team. A fire they set went awry, he died, but she is holding onto his ghost. He is trying to convince her to let him go, find peace in the hereafter, and get herself a new life where she can find a partnership as special as the one that he had with her mother.*

## H

She was troubled in a way nobody can fix, Littles. You just live with what you're given. If there's more on the way, well, You just can't know. But you got to try. Your mother and I, there was a time where I … I'd lived all my life in the heat. A child raised in fire. Living with, above, life. Skimming across the top. The unwaking world. There was the first time I saw her … But there was a space of time from when I took my first breath to when I really started breathing. That moment that usually lasts five seconds for ever'body else, Lasted 16 years for me. I mean, I knew how to get dressed and eat and sleep and lay fuses and diffuse the smell of gasoline. I did do the, the things you do. The waking life things. But it was, mechanical, A machine of a boy, A machine of a man, Not breathing. Not living. There was a terrible completeness to it. Which in the back of my mechanical mind equaled life. A to B to C to D to E to F to end of day to end of night to end of morning to end of afternoon. The completeness we're told makes you full, takes life life. We'd weave and measure and cut and pretend to be the fates. But really, There was a coldness, Littles, A chill that just, froze inside me, kept me from really breathing. I'd stand in the warm afternoon rain not knowing why but craving the thaw. The first time I touched her hand, pretending it was an accident, brushed my fingers over hers at the market, reaching for a grocery bag, I started gasping like a fish just reeled in on the boat. I dropped to my knees and thought I was going to die. Thought this is what it must feel like to be trapped in a blaze that won't ever turn over and burn out. Thought this is it. The cut. But she knelt down with me and took both my hands and we breathed together. And that was my first breath, Doodlebug, My honest to God first. And when we rose up together, I was a new man. I was 16 and just born and that was it. I think you've been born, Littles, but you don't breathe. You don't live like how your momma did for me. You haven't started breathing yet. There's something in that. But there's also something beyond. A fire in yourself so deep that you can't reach it without someone else. I'm not talking about sex. It's more intimate. A release, from yourself to yourself, That takes someone else's love to ignite. Otherwise you burn cold, no air, no breath, to feed the flames, Get you alive. Clotho. Lachesis. Atropos. That's your momma, Littles. That's who your Momma was to me. Clotho – creator of my life. Lachesis – measure of my life. Atropos – my final destiny. Now I'm going to go be with her, You have to help me be with her. And then you need to go off on your own. Find your own breath, 'cause you haven't taken your first yet, Littles. Not by any measure. And you can't do that with me here. Bury me whole and leave this place. Lay down the burden of us; stop lettin' us bear you down.

# BARBECUE APOCALYPSE

*Matt Lyle*

Seriocomic
Win, thirties

*Pre-Apocalypse: Win, a middle-upper management corporate cog and legend in his own mind, gives his artistic friend, Mike, a pep talk.*

## WIN

You have to aim higher, man. You can't shrug, "Oh, things are fine, fine, I'll just pick my nose. That'll be fine." You're a medium. Like small, medium, large. I'm a large. You're medium. Like, homeless people are smalls. I might be a extra-large. Go big or go home, Mike. You gotta live by that. I am trying to help you, ass. If something you want presents itself what do you do? You pussy think about it. You weigh your pussy options. You look at it from both pussy sides and then you do something pussy safe and everything is pussy fine. Something I want presents itself and I punch it in the dick, throw it over my shoulder, laugh all the way home. I'm a business man, Mike. I do business. I make deals with the most powerful people in this city on a daily basis. A daily fucking basis, Mike. You know what I'm saying? No room for compromise. Cut throat. All I can worry about is my six figures. Fuck everybody else. You've got to get Ayn Rand on this bitch. Get it? Confidence, Mike. You've got no confidence. That's why you're okay with things being fine. I've got confidence that I could have anything I want so I end up getting it. You know what I'm saying?

For information on this author,
click on the WRITERS tab at www.smithandkraus.com.

# BARBECUE APOCALYPSE
## Matt Lyle

Dramatic
Win, thirties

*Post-Apocalypse: Win hasn't fared well after the apocalypse and his girlfriend has very recently kidnapped by a very bad man. The group of survivors, who were all friends before the apocalypse, are considering reaching out to another group of survivors. They all cast their votes. This is Win's vote.*

### WIN

They'll trick us, guys! They'll trick us. They'll tell us- Lulu- Lulu, they'll tell us they have dildos that you plug into the wall if that's what you want to hear. They'll take us in and talk to us about...about survival and then they'll take the only thing that we've ever had that has been real, that's been important, the only thing we've ever truly earned. They'll leave us broken. Everything we thought about ourselves before the apocalypse was all wrong. Then just as we were coming to terms with who we thought we were now...it'll just get ripped away from us again. I'm not sure we'll have anything to live for. The darkness that has been outside will finally swallow us. The darkness that we used to keep at bay with money, and sex, and pride, and...and feeling big, feeling strong, feeling successful, and cars, and where we lived, and how much better we were doing than the people we measured ourselves against. Now we only have candles and our wits. Both so easily snuffed. Make no mistake, the darkness will wash over us, inky, black, choking...It will be the...true end of us.

For information on this author,
click on the WRITERS tab at www.smithandkraus.com.

# BARBECUE APOCALYPSE
## *Matt Lyle*

Dramatic
John, thirties-fifties

*Post-Apocalypse: John, an evil man, has tracked down a group of survivors and aims to take everything they have. He fondly remembers discovering his true nature.*

## JOHN

You are some chatty sons of bitches. I had something to do: stay alive. And it suited me, I guess, cuz I'm still doing it. This may be the longest I've sat still in...months. No, I'm always moving now. Always hunting. Can I be honest with you all? I think I can. Cuz I know Win here and he told me all about you, except where you were. Friends taking care of each other. It's nice. You remind me of me and my friends a little. Lemme tell you a story. A short story. I had fallen in with these folks in Atlanta, or outside of Atlanta. Four of us guys; Me, Jim, Ted, Michael, all looking out for each other. Buddies. God, Ted was funny as hell. Even in the face of all this. Always good for...for a laugh. Man, I loved Ted. Anyway, we were traveling and following every rumor about safe places and...we were dying. We were wasting away. And I was in my sleeping bag one night. Looking up at the sky and figuring it was my last night to see it. And...I was thinking back to the man I was before...Always wanting, but never doing anything about it... and then I looked at my situation, dying, scared, hungry. And then I was truthful to myself, about myself for the first time. I figured out who I really was and how I fit into this world. That's real happiness. I just stood right up and I put my hand over Ted's mouth and I stuck my knife right into his neck. And it worked like that for the others, too. Their eyes went wide then just out. In two minutes I was alone. Then I took everything they had that I needed. It hadn't been enough for the four of us. But it was enough for me. Your friend here, Win... he's kind of a douche bag. You probably all know that, right? I came across him and that sweet, sweet...Glory. Perfect name. And she had something I needed. I could see they were both as soft as tissue paper but he let me know that he was a business man and wanted to make a deal. So, I made him a couple of offers. I wouldn't kill him and I get the girl. Or I could kill him and I'd get the girl. He jumped at that first one. So, I walked outta there with a real woman. Neither would tell me where you all were. So, I just followed his dumbass over here. And low and behold...two more women. An embarrassment of riches. OK? Everybody understand the situation? I'm going to kill you fellas. Sorry, I don't need you. Then me and the ladies will take all your nice stuff, load it into my van out front and split.

For information on this author,
click on the WRITERS tab at www.smithandkraus.com.

Lawrence Harbison

# BAR BY THE F

*Sheila Callaghan*

Seriocomic
Young Man, twenties

*A young, skittish, highly nerdy man sits in a bar, fantasizing about the female bartender.*

## YOUNG MAN

I'm here tonight because my regular bar is renovating *(again)* and right now I want to be telling you about how this city continues to break me in the smallest and fakest of ways but it won't happen because really I'm a COWARD though I think you'd understand about things like kismet with all its itchiness and sorcery. AND I noticed you aren't facing those dudes you keep taking to, you like peep from the sides of your eyes like an old-timey Hollywood dame… yeah it's devicey and cheap but I am still in love with you for it, and heck I have a wardrobe filled with thrift-store gestures too and I want to show them all to you. I only live a block from here.

*A beat. He pounds on his laptop.*

COWARD COWARD COWARD COWARD COWARD. Ultimately it's about gratitude anyway, right, I should feel gratitude for being allowed to look at you like this because it's stealing in a way, me sipping you like a secret beverage. and ultimately I should be GRATEFUL for your lack of knowledge because it keeps me safe. I like being safe, it's why I bring my laptop to bars. So yes. I am grateful that you will never ever talk to me.

*He glances up. He blushes and hides behind his screen, typing madly.*

You just glanced at me again— third time in twelve minutes WHY CAN'T I HANG ONTO THE GAZE sink my teeth in like a rabid dog. Please come lean over me in your tank top ask me if I want another drink I have a ream of secrets I want to embroider into your scalp I'll use a special needle made from songs my parents sang to me and thread made from the sweetest parts of my youth and the darkest parts of my early twenties. I can't see your feet behind the bar but I imagine you are wearing like feminista cowboy boots that kind of ironic screw-you-redneck thing, you have a short skirt with little tiny flowers it's vintage like maybe your mother wore it at her first summer picnic and beneath are your PANTIES PANTIES PANTIES . I imagine you in pink cotton boy-briefs holy mama and you have a tank top on even though it's November but I guess it gets stuffy in here with the windows shut god I didn't even realize it's raining and anyway you are running around an awful lot back there waiting on those guys MAN I hate those guys. HEY look at me, a white hot beam of foolishness and flushed pirate dreams connects us, it draws us very very slowly slowly to one another... or it could... maybe... if you just...

Things I want to nibble. A list. By me.

1. your sun-colored bangs
2. the way you don't face people when you talk to them
3. Your blue tights
4. Your hair (You've put it up twice and down twice)
5. your shoulder tattoo, is that dice?
6. one more Jameson
7. your hair
8. Your tank top
9. Your ...

---

# THE BELLE OF BELMAR

*Nicole Pandolfo*

Dramatic
Mikey, seventeen

*Mikey's two buddies raped Denise while she was drunk. He was the only witness. They got away with it because Denise did not file charges. Denise has found a video on his phone of the rape, and has confronted him about his failure to tell anyone about it.*

## MIKEY

They said you begged them. And then they told me not to tell anyone, but then they went and told people anyway. Coach found out about it too. And he asked them about it. He asked them questions about it for like, fifteen minutes. They even delayed practice …And they told him that you were into it. But that they regretted it because their girlfriends got mad at them. And that they just wanted to forget about it. And they did. Everyone forgot about it. That night. You were supposed to sleep over. I was gonna give you the top bunk, remember. You kept drinking so much with Brad and Colby. I didn't drink anything. I didn't drink then. Goldschlagger. It smelled so gross. But you kept drinking it. I've never seen you drink like that before. And then all the sudden it was late and I was tired. I tried to get you to come upstairs with me because you were gonna sleep in the top bunk. You were slurring. I kept telling you to come, but you wouldn't come. You wouldn't move. You were drunk. Passed out. And Brad and Colby were asleep on the floor so I went up to bed. And then a while later I heard something weird and when I came downstairs… If I would have argued with Brad and Colby about it they could have got in trouble. Kicked off the team. I could have got kicked off the team. We're not supposed to drink. And then all the best players would be gone and we'd have lost all the big games and who knows, I might not be getting into the kinda schools I'll probably get into, and my mom and dad would have never talked to me again and everyone in school would have hated me.

For information on this author,
click on the WRITERS tab at www.smithandkraus.com.

# BIG CITY

## Barbara Blumenthal-Ehrlich

Seriocomic
Joe, twenties-thirties

*Joe is talking to his roommate-with-benefits, Jane. He feels alone and swallowed up by the city and wants to kick their relationship up several notches by having a baby together. Joe makes his "baby" pitch when Jane is immobilized with a strained back. Even in her vulnerable state, she refuses, claiming to be different than Joe. Here, he explains how similar they really are.*

### JOE

It's fine. I'm fine. I've always been this way. Four brushes of each tooth. Eight sips of my coffee before my bagel. Twelve steps in the subway car... It's how I beat the flu season. It's how I got into college. And made varsity and got my horrible, nightmare job. It works. Just, not today. We have something. You and me. This morning, seeing you lying there on the couch, I saw my opening— I did hide the remote... and everything else. I wanted you unplugged and disconnected from all the distracting, deadening... stuff that keeps you from seeing what I see. From knowing what I know. What we have doesn't come along every day. Maybe just once in a lifetime. What are you waiting for? If Prince Charming was coming, he'd have been here by now. So you were alone today. Big deal. You think that's any different than—You go to work in a taxi – alone. You sit in your office 12 hours a day – alone. You eat – alone. Meetings? Conference calls? Business lunches? I watch that whole corner office scene. You're just as alone as me. I don't mean to make you feel bad... I just see things shifting with us. Sunday mornings we made love. Two months of Sundays. Not a "couple." When was the last time you went on a date? When, since we started this "arrangement" – in the last, what, year or whatever – have you or I been out with anyone else? What if I'm your prince? And *that's* what scares you? Jane. Talk to me. You know what your problem is? Your life is "out there" in the future somewhere – after Mr. Right, the house, kids, corner office, whatever. It can't be me and you because first "this" has to happen and "that" has to fall into place. It's never here. It's never now. It's all on hold until tomorrow. As if there's even going to be a tomorrow anymore. Who knows?

For information on this author,
click on the WRITERS tab at www.smithandkraus.com.

# BIG SKY

## *Alexandra Gersten-Vassilaros*

Dramatic
Jack, mid to late-forties

*Snaring the job of a lifetime, Jack has just shared the good news with Jonathan, his wife Jen's friend. Now that his jangled nerves about the job have been calmed, he leans in to get some other important questions answered. He is concerned about the state of his marriage and, with a couple glasses of wine under his belt, feels free enough to confess his most intimate problems with Jonathan, which has likely never happened before.*

### JACK

Oh yeah? How many years in a phase - you know, approximately? I'm only asking because a few, a few years ago she comes home, right, and announces that the reason she has no sex drive is *not* because of me. How can having no sex drive *not* have something to do with me if I'm the one who's never going to have sex again, right? Because a man, a *man* needs sex to stay balanced. We require it, it's not even a preference, it's a goddamned health issue! And if your wife comes home and announces that sex, good, bad or in between, is virtually over, what's a man supposed to do? It worries me because is she saying that from now on it's a closed shop? I dunno. I dunno. Maybe marriage was a better idea when life expectancy was lower. I'm telling you, she's freaking me out, especially because if I bring it up, I've committed the terrible unforgivable act of not understanding her. And guess what? I don't! But I have to act like I do! And to be totally honest, there was never even that much sex anyway, not since Tessa was born. And then with trying and trying to have a second one, two rounds of IVF treatments, I mean, that'll take the fun out of sex right there…and you know, the last few years I've had my own fucking problems so…

*(He trails off for a moment.)*

But when we did have it, it was good, I mean, no complaints there, it was great. She was great. I love her. How could I not?

For information on this author,
click on the WRITERS tab at www.smithandkraus.com.

# BIRDS OF A FEATHER

*June Guralnik*

Comic
AP Wells, thirties

*AP's study, 2018. AP Wells is a British-schooled, time-travelling scientist/genius with a quirky sense of humor and fascination for toys, magic, and mysteries. A bit of a Casanova. Suffers from sciurophobia (fear of squirrels). Since returning to his own time, he has been pining for Diana Katherine Birdwhistle. The problem – Diana lived more than a hundred years ago. AP directly addresses the audience.*

## AP

Exactly one hundred and five years since my head first collided with Diana's. My trip through time was supposed to be easy-peasy. No muss, no fuss, no rockin' history's feathers!

*(He air guitars to a rock tune.)*

Pull it together, man! You're in love with a 130 year old woman – how will that play on the six o'clock tellie?! On the plus side, we're a shoe-in for the Guinness Book's strangest couple, hands-down beating the gay penguins in the San Francisco Zoo and that 58-hour kissing couple - who didn't even pause their lip-smacking to use the commode! I'm sponsoring a new Guinness prize in their honor – "Couple with the Most Infectious Germs!"

*(Looks down at his crotch.)*

The thrill is gone! This is what I've come to! AP, you're at the pinnacle of your career. Your Sherlock Holmes sex game has sold five million copies! And bringing back a species from extinction isn't too shabby either!

*(Takes out phone and calls Stephen Hawkins.)*

Stephen Hawkins – hello, old chap. Quick question if you have a millisecond. If, as Steinhardt suggests, the entire visible universe is a 3-brine –

*(to audience)*

a three dimensional membrane embedded in a larger structure -

*(Returns to call.)*

Then is it possible an infinite number of separate parallel universes – parallel brines, if you will - exist? Uh huh. Fantastic! Thanks!

*(to audience)*

Let's skip the lecture about upsetting the space-time apple cart. I'm simply making a teensy, weensy adjustment in one itty bitty brine. For all we know, in a parallel universe Lady Gaga is a hostess at Waffle House and Hilary Clinton has replaced Trump on Celebrity Apprentice. We are all living multiple lives on other planes… one big funhouse mirror, right?

# BREATHING TIME

## Beau Willimon

Seriocomic
Jack, late twenties-thirties

*Jack works in the marketing department of an architectural firm. At the start of his day he's chatting with another guy in his department about this and that instead of working. Here, he tells the other guy about a shit job he had the summer after his freshman year of college, working as a toilet seat inspector in a plastics factory.*

### JACK

Toilet seat would come outta the machine every eight and a half seconds. Twelve hours a day. Five-fifteen AM to five-fifteen PM. And when I got off my shift at five-fifteen PM a dude would take over at my machine and work twelve hours until I showed up again at five-fifteen AM. Joint ran twenty-four hours a day, seven days a week. Totally de-sensitized. Earplugs. Gloves. Safety glasses. No human contact. Not even a fuckin window in the place. Had to get permission from the foreman to use the  bathroom so he could take over your machine while you were takin a piss. Almost drove me crazy it was so fuckin boring. At first I'd bring in books, set them up next to the conveyor belt.  Would read one sentence in between each part. One sentence at a time every eight and half seconds. Got through a lot of heavy German shit – Thomas Mann, Gunter Grass... Anyway, one day my foreman comes up to me, says "Jack, I don't know what you're doin with those books, but you're bein paid to inspect parts, not to read." So *then*, I started bringin in a little note-pad and in-between each part I'd play little games to keep myself from goin bonkers. Would see how quick I could write down all fifty states. New Hampshire, New York, New Jersey. Inspect a part. North Dakota, South Dakota, Maine. Inspect a part. Or how fast I could write down all the presidents. Washington, Adams, Jefferson. Or write down new lyrics to songs, like (*singing to the tune of the Beatles' "Yesterday)* "Just last May, I wasn't inspecting parts all day. If I quit I wonder what my Mom would say..." Well *then* my foreman comes up to me and says "Jack – I don't know what you're doin with that notepad, but you're here to inspect parts, not scribble in some book." Just turned my brain off for the rest of the summer and (*in a deep dramatic voice*) became one with the machine.

For information on this author,
click on the WRITERS tab at www.smithandkraus.com.

Lawrence Harbison

# BREATHING TIME

*Beau Willimon*

Dramatic
Jack, thirties

*Jack works in the marketing department of an architectural firm. Here, he tells another guy in his office about the bad gambling night he had.*

## JACK

Why I was out so late. Spent the whole fuckin night tryin to make back the money I lost. Half of it on one hand too. I had a fuckin straight and Benny – you know Benny, right? Book-runner over in the middle-office? Benny throws down a fuckin full house. And a pussy full-house too. Fours full of eights. Poof. Hundred and fifty down the drain. Whatever. I'll win it back next week. See, most of these guys, granted, they're decent players. They're good with numbers. Can work out all the odds in their head, all the probabilities. But they're transparent as a fuckin glass of water. Gino – he's got a chip on his shoulder. So all you gotta do with him is wait for a halfway respectable hand and re-raise the fuck out of him. Ted? He's nothin but math. So when he's bettin you know he's gonna win. But the rest he'll lay down if so much breathe in his direction. And Benny – he's just a spineless son of bitch. You can bluff his ass any day of the week. Dude was *born* with his tail between his legs. I'm telling you – these guys don't *get* it. Think they can read each other, but they're lookin for a twitch of an eye or someone tappin his foot. That's just white noise. What you gotta *do* is convince yourself you can hear a guy's heart beating. Tap into the rhythms. Smell the sweat under his skin before it even reaches the pores. Play the *man* instead of the odds. Then it doesn't even matter what his cards are.

For information on this author,
click on the WRITERS tab at www.smithandkraus.com.

# BREATHING TIME

*Beau Willimon*

Seriocomic
Jack, thirties

*Jack tells a co-worker about a money-making scheme he's come up with.*

## JACK

It's a pretty simple idea. You trade against the ratings so if they come up short on a show we make up the difference on what an company paid for advertising that didn't reach its projected audience. But we charge a fee, so if the ratings match their projections we walk away with a profit. And we can play both sides. The networks can insure themselves the same way. If the rating exceed their projections then we make up the difference on the revenue they lost from underselling their rates. I'm a fuckin artist – I bank with imagination. You know how the big catchword this year from the top is "Innovation," right? It's all about new this, new that. New new new new new. Okay, so all the traders are runnin around tryin to come up with new invest-ment schemes. New ways to split a billion up into all these compli-cated investment models that will turn a dime. And I figure there's no way I'm gonna be able to compete with them on that. I mean, I got my finger on the market's pulse, but these dudes got their dicks plugged into the aorta. So I say to myself, fuck new *investments*, let's find ourself a new *market*. And at first I'm thinkin somethin overseas – some piece of shit third world country we can ram some oil drills into or some shit like that. But I don't know fuck all about geopolitical resources and all that crap. So I'm up against a brick wall. Then I'm watchin the Yanks play the Sox on TV and I'm and wonderin if the Sox might actually make it to the Series this year and if they *did* how every fuckin household in America will tune in and how much a thirty second ad of commercials will cost a fortune and it fuckin hits me. We place bets on everything else. Why not place bets on how many knuckleheads'll tune into a Sox game, or the Miss America Contest, or the Oscars, or whatever? So I write up a one page memo. Send it to the VP of marketing. He loves it. Sends it up to the C.O.O. C.double O loves it. Sends it up to the Board. Next thing I know I got a twenty percent raise and a meeting with the Big

Lawrence Harbison

Dicks in... (*looking at his watch*) … roughly twenty-eight minutes.


For information on this author,
click on the WRITERS tab at www.smithandkraus.com.

# CAL IN CAMO

## William Francis Hoffman

Seriocomic
Tim, thirties

*Tim, a desperate beer rep from the Bridgeport section of Chicago, is trying to sell the exotically flavored craft beer that worked for him in the city to an uninterested old tavern owner in rural Illinois.*

### TIM

Look here's the deal...it ain't about what's in there or what's not in there...or how it tastes or how it looks...or makes you look...you don't have to like it at all...you don't have to taste it you don't have to smell it see it...or give a damn at all...but I'm telling you what it does... what I've seen it do...it's about people...it's about knowin' people... you gotta trust me on this...it's magic this beer...I've seen it turn bars around...I've seen it turn lives around...girls hate beer...it smells like their dad...it tastes like cereal without the sugar...they think it makes em' look fat...but this...this they love...cause it's not like a beer at all... it's like a kiss...it's like a giggle...this is for them...it ain't for us...it's for them...and where are we we're right behind them with our wallets open...we can't help ourselves ...cause they're smilin'...and we'll pay for that smile all night...it lights em' up and they light up the room and before you know it...you have the place people wanna be...this brings in the girls...the girls bring in the guys and the guys bring their wallets...and suddenly you have the place you always wanted...I'm just like you...I'm a regular guy same as you ... don't let the tie fool you and all this...I grew up on the southside of chicago my dad was a city cop fought his way through the ranks and made captain...I used ta do a little bartending even myself...I come from regular people... but I took a chance on this stuff...because it was different ...because it was odd...because it was like nothing I'd ever tasted before...but it worked...it worked for me...and it can work for you...I know you didn't put four bar stools in here...cause ya liked em' empty. *(a shift)* I got a newborn...and a house...and a wife...and it's hot and my head is poundin'...my head is poundin' and I'm not sayin' that...to get any kinda a you know...I'm just sayin'...I've been hearin' nothin' but no all day...how bout you be my first yes...how bout you be my guy...I got a feelin' about you...tell you what just take a six pack...take one for free and just pass it around see what it gets ya...see if I'm not right... see if I don't know what I'm talkin' about.

For information on this author,
click on the WRITERS tab at www.smithandkraus.com.

# CAL IN CAMO
## *William Francis Hoffman*

Dramatic
Flynt, thirties

*Flynt is a grieving, newly widowed hunter from St. Genevieve, Missouri, who is deeply connected to nature. He lost his wife in a flood because he wasn't able to hold on to her, and is begging for forgiveness from his furious sister as he tries explain where he disappeared to in the middle of the night.*

### FLYNT

I ain't doin' shit to you... I ain't doin' shit to nobody...I was sittin' out there mindin' my own damn business..I musta fallen asleep.. casue when I woke up it was pourin'...I mean pourin'...sky just opend the fuck up..I knew it was comin'....and I see that doe way out there in the moonlight right in the middle a them bradfords..and she's lookin' at me she knows I see her even from that distance. So I grab the rifle and I start to go out there and I'm fightin' through the rain fightin' through the brush and I'm makin' a helluva noise..and she shoulda been gone she shoulda took the fuck off but she don't she don't move an inch and when I finally get out there far enough and get inside that ring of bradfords I see why she ain't movin'..you have no idea what your dealin' with out there it's huge it's the biggest damn sink hole I've ever seen waters rushin' into it from all sides.. and she's waist deep in that water...she takes a step that water's gonna pull her right into the ground and she knows it....and she's cryin' cause she knows it...I can feel it...I feel her cryin'...I can feel it in my chest..it's rattlin' my bones ...and she's shakin' I can see her shakin'....and I raise the rifle...and I'm tryin' to steady myself in the water...tryin' to take aim.. tryin' to get her right where I need to....and just as I'm about to pull the trigger...she takes a step and boom she goes under and I drop the rifle and I start runnin'...runnin' along the side where there's still ground to run and she pops back up but the water's takin' her fast and I start runnin' out into the water and it's gettin' deeper as I'm runnin'.. and she's comin' toward me and so I dive under I put my whole body under the water..and I wait for her to come to me...and when she does boom I snatch her up like this from underneath boom like this hard both my arms under her arms..and her chest hits my chest boom chest to chest just like this and I start pushin' and she's kickin' like hell hard against the water.. 'n I'm holdin' her while I'm fightin'... movin' us toward the edge of those bradfords..and I'm pushin' and pushin' and boom.... I slam her up against the roots... I push us up outta the water and I wrap my arms around the tree and push my body hard up against hers just like I shoulda..and I grab on to the roots with my hands tight like I shoulda...tight this time...like I shoulda and I got my face next to her face.. and I'm smellin' her breath and her fur and I'm lookin in her eye and I am not lettin' go this time no matter what I am not lettin' go..and she got still in my arms....she let me hold her like that....she didn't fight or kick or nuthin'...and the water kept comin'...up to my chest and my neck and my mouth and just as I was about to lose my space to breathe the rain stopped ..and the water backed off and the trees closed in and when I finally saw the ground beneath me when I saw my knees in the mud and my body draped over hers and saw her legs and her body solid on the ground.........I let go......and I stood up and then she stood up and instead of takin' off she comes toward me like this she got right up close to my face like this... and it was Annabelle's face...and her eyes were Annabelle's eyes ..and I could smell her breath..and it was Annabelle's breath she got real close to my face like this real close...and then boom she took off like a shot boom...running and leapin' through the woods......leapin' over rocks... you shoulda seen her go....boom...she takes off...weavin' in and outta trees splashin' water up under her feet...and I watched her go I watched her go until I couldn't see her anymore...until she was gone..she was so fast you shoulda seen her and she ain't never been a deer before and she knew just how to do it.............why'd she do that look at me like that...right in the eye like that..why'd she do that........

# CARBON-BASED LIFE FORM SEEKS SIMILAR
## Andrew Biss

Comic
Mr. Loveworth, could be any age

*Mr. Loveworth, the owner of a dating agency, is speaking to a potential client.*

### MR. LOVEWORTH

Look, Leslie, I'm trying to help you achieve your goals, but if I'm to do so, you're going to have to confront some uncomfortable truths. Now, in Prehistoric times, things were much more straightforward. You could simply wrap yourself in a pelt, grunt a few times at your heart's desire and live happily ever after. These days things are a little more complicated. Every aspect of your being has to be cultivated and contrived. Nothing can be left to chance. The way you dress, the way you walk, the way you smile, the way you talk, all of it has to be manufactured with absolute precision in order to create the *real* you – the one that closes the deal. Then and only then will you have become something truly viable in today's fickle and uncertain market. Let me put it this way. Let's say I send you out to meet with a very nice gentleman who you find yourself very attracted to, and the next evening you anxiously await his call. He, meanwhile, that very same evening, is enjoying cocktails with friends who are all eager to hear the outcome of his first date, and to whom he relays any one of the following: "She redefined the word dull." "From the way she dressed I assumed she was manic depressive" "Her hair kept reminding me of my grandmother." "She was nice enough, but God, that annoying laugh!" Or perhaps, "In a million years I could *never* get used to that nose."

(*Beat*)

Do you see what I mean? Incidentally, *your* nose – have you considered surgery?

# CHILL

*Eleanor Burgess*

Dramatic
Stu, eighteen

*In the midst of a fun night drinking beers and catching up with his friends, Stu finds himself alone with Jenn, seventeen, one of the nerdier girls in their friend group, and opens up to her about a major choice that's hanging over his head - one that will decide a lot about his future before he's even gotten out of high school.*

## STU

I got into Florida State. Yeah. But I'm waiting to hear back from Duke. And if I do get in, I only have a week to decide. To my parents it is. But there's this pitching coach. At Florida State. And he's like – he's good. He's really good. For curveball especially. I mean he's a fucking weirdo. I can't understand his accent and he pops gum constantly when he talks. But he coached Jack Desko. You know him? He's with the Braves. He coached Emilio Betancourt and – I can't remember, a bunch of guys. Pros. And I have this decision. I can cash it in, ride the arm, get a Duke degree, and that's something, that's really fucking something. But I just wonder – with the right coach, with the right team. And it's hanging over my head all day, like- I try to focus in class, or when I'm hanging out, or whatever, but the whole time I'm just thinking, "Am I good enough? Am I good enough?" I run through every minute of practice in my head, like, I nail a pitch, I'm good enough, I'm late on a play, I'm not good enough. Every night I have to decide, like, do my homework or practice more, and I don't want to fail Spanish. But *if I'm good enough...*

# CHILL

## *Eleanor Burgess*

Dramatic
Ethan, twenty-seven

*Ethan is catching up with old high school friends who are back in town for Thanksgiving. He's endured some good-natured teasing from his well-off best friend about his lack of serious relationships and his extreme left-wing political beliefs - then he learns his well-off best friend voted Republican in a recent election, and the teasing doesn't seem so fun anymore.*

## ETHAN

I spend my days reading about possible apocalypses. I run models of what will happen when temperatures rise, when we won't be able to grow corn anymore, when we won't be able to grow rice, and when we'll all be in a world war over food, and how are we going to support tropical refugees with diminished agricultural resources? I read about when water supplies will give out, and whether desalinization will let us get enough water from the ocean, and how much energy it will take to do that desalinization, and how that energy use will contribute to further warming. And I read about whether maybe we won't need as much food, because there could be a plague of antibioticresistant bacteria, or small pox, or a nuclear disaster. And I think about Fukushima, and Deepwater Horizon. And I try to figure out whether there's a way to prevent all of this, through carbon scrubbing and fusion technology, and then I think about how we've known about this for thirty years!! And I don't really know why it all couldn't have gone better. There's no reason why it all couldn't have gone better, if people had just *tried* harder, and I think about that, I spend eight to ten hours a day thinking about that, nice weather makes me think about dying, so sorry if I don't want to spend my life in a way that even you admit is boring as fuck, and have three children who I firmly believe are going to e condemned to a lifetime of violent warfare over food supplies, and I don't want to send out cute little save the dates where my leggy fiancée and I frolic with our border collie on our poisonously large suburban lawn that could absorb 100 times as much $CO_2$ if only we could get off our butts long enough to plant some fucking trees.

Lawrence Harbison

# CONSIDER THE OYSTER

## David MacGregor

Seriocomic
Gene Walsh, twenties.

*Upon learning that he is transforming into a woman due to a medical*
*accident, Gene attempts to break up with his fiancée without telling her*
*the truth about what is happening to him.*

### GENE

Marisa, there's something I need to tell you. I can't marry you. And no,
it's not another woman…or man. It's…okay, you deserve an explana-
tion. You deserve the complete and honest truth, so I'm just going to
say this straight out. I can't marry you because I'm…I'm a schmuck.
A total, goofball, idiot loser. I am. I see that now. I mean, I gave you
a pretzel as an engagement ring. I didn't put any time or thought into
it. I didn't think about what kind of stone or setting you might like. I
didn't take you out to a romantic restaurant or a moonlit beach. I just
gave you a salty snack because I was excited about a football game.
That's pathetic. Because I'm pathetic. And I don't deserve someone
as beautiful and wonderful as you. I don't deserve anyone until I
grow up a little. You want to know the truth about me? Well, here it
is. I don't like French Country kitchens. And I don't like Yorkshire
terriers. And I don't like shopping for antiques. There. You see? I'm
a fraud! A complete and total fraud! I'm a poser. A faker. I'm not the
person you think I am and we never really had that much in common.
Sooner or later, you'd have realized that. You're the straight A student
going out with the class loser. The purebred going out with the mutt.
It might seem like a good idea right now, but that wouldn't last! It'd
be that same old story you see again and again. The train leaves Love
Station full of hope and desire, but then somehow, somewhere along
the way, the train jumps the tracks and you end up in Hate City. And
you look at the person you used to love with all your heart, the person
you wanted to spend the rest of your life with, and you can't understand
what you ever saw in them in the first place. And I don't want that to
happen. I don't want you to wind up hating me. Because I love you.
I love you more than I ever thought I could love anyone. In fact, you
know what? If I didn't love you as much as I do, I'd marry you tomor-

row! I would! I'd figure what the hell, Marisa's a good starter wife, let's give it a shot. But I don't want that for us. I don't want that for you. More than anything, I want you to be happy. And you wouldn't be happy with me. I guarantee you, the day would come when you would look at me and say to yourself, "This is not the Gene I fell in love with. This is not the Gene I want to be with." And I don't think I could stand knowing that was happening. Marisa, I know this is out of the blue and everything, but it's for the best. It really is. It may not seem like it, but we're really pretty lucky…lucky that we went our own ways…while we're still in love.

For information on this author,
click on the WRITERS tab at www.smithandkraus.com.

Lawrence Harbison

# THE COWARD

## Kati Schwartz

Comic
Christopher, twenty-three

*Christopher is a charming social genius, confident of the control he has over everyone but himself. His identity is greatly affected by his deeply religious upbringing. Here, he speaks to a new friend, for whom he has unfamiliar romantic feelings.*

### CHRISTOPHER

Not only are you poly-amorous and bisexual, but you just said you were an atheist? What is that like? I always have this image of atheists just being super *weird*. Like burning shit all the time. I mean, just whenever I think of an atheist, I think of weird hippies like, burning sage and sacrificing animals, and like, rolling around in blood. Oh my GOSH I'm totally kidding! But yeah, you're right. Christians did used to burn women who they thought were witches. I'm just saying. There's more stuff than just what's in The Crucible. Like, I know that a lot of lesbians were burned. Arthur Miller never even mentions that. Lesbians did used to be considered witches, though. Truly, I would not make this up. Like, people thought it was so unnatural for two people of the same gender to kiss or anything, that they would just instantly be killed if they were caught. *(Pause)* I don't really blame the people who did it, to be honest. That sounds way worse than I meant for it to. I just mean, like, what if they had actually turned out to be real witches, who were like, casting spells all over the place? Like, for example, let's say your grandma died. Just out of nowhere. She wasn't sick or anything, and she just *died.* How could you prove that some witch didn't just cast a death spell on her to, like, get you back for something you did? Especially back in those times. That would freak me out.

For information on this author,
click on the WRITERS tab at www.smithandkraus.com.

# DANIEL'S HUSBAND

## Michael McKeever

Dramatic
Daniel, forties

*Daniel, a gay architect, describes to the audience - in chilling detail - the events leading up to the stroke which has left him a quadriplegic, unable to speak, but still cognitive and fully aware of what is happening around him.*

### DANIEL

Cerebromedullospinal Disconnection. *(beat)* When you say it slow like that, it sounds almost pretty, right? Here. Let's make it easy and put it in layman's terms: Locked-in Syndrome. So much better. You know - completely descriptive, right to the point. It's typically caused by a blockage in the part of the brainstem that acts as a bridge between brain and body. The part that controls the nerves that are used for . . . well, pretty much everything we do on a day-to-day basis: Walking, talking, the works. The most common cause is a blood clot. A stroke. Which is what I had: A brainstem stroke. The result: Quadriplegia and the inability to speak in an otherwise cognitively intact individual. In other words, I am completely conscious and aware – I know everything that is happening around me - despite the fact that I cannot move, I cannot talk, I cannot communicate in any way.

*(Beat. He surveys the audience to confirm that they understand.)*

So this is what happens. This is how it works. You get this headache. Not particularly bad. You've had worse. And you're having a fight with your partner. It's a fight you've had before. And then suddenly there's a . . . I don't know . . . a loud buzzing sound in your ears. Something that's never happened before. And you can just tell it's something serious. Something not good. And then there's this click. Like a loud snapping sound. And you feel something inside of you break. And you tell your partner to call 911. And as he's on the phone with them, you start to tell him that he needs to calm down, only nothing comes out of your mouth. In fact, your mouth isn't even moving. The words are forming in your brain, but your mouth won't say them. And suddenly your knees are buckling and you're falling to the ground and your partner is running to you. And now he's really panicking. And you want to hug him and let him know that it's going to be okay, that together you will work this out. But you realize your arms aren't working. It's not like they're numb. You can feel them. You can feel everything. The cold of the tiles on your skin. His warm breath on your face. His tears. You just can't move. Anything. *(beat) Anything.* And now he's back on the phone. And he's screaming at someone. You see him across the room on the phone and he is terrified. And it hurts you to see him so scared. And you want to turn away . . . but you can't, because you can't move. And you don't close your eyes. Because . . . because you are afraid if you close your eyes, you will die. And now he's turning you on your back. Apparently the person on the phone has told him to do this. He says something about airways and breathing. He asks if you can hear him. And you want to scream YES, of course I can hear you. But you can't. And the tile is so cold. And his breath is so warm. And he's squeezing you hand. And you can't squeeze it back. And you start to understand just how bad this is. I mean, you don't *really* understand what is happening or why your body is doing what it's doing. But for the first time, you begin to get an idea of what your life is about to become. *(beat)* And somewhere in the distance, you hear the ambulance. And you know it's coming for you. But you don't close your eyes. Because, if you close your eyes . .

# DANIEL'S HUSBAND
## Michael McKeever

Seriocomic
Trip, early twenties

*Trip, a gay in-home healthcare specialist, tries to cheer up a patient with the story of a disastrous first date with a 40 year old ex-Mormon.*

### TRIP

Now then. Where was I? *Right.* The Ex-Mormon. So, I'm on this first date with this Mormon. This *Ex*-Mormon. Have you ever noticed that there are a lot of gay Ex-Mormons? Anyway, he's somewhere in his early 40's. And kind of cute, I guess. I've done worse. And we're driving along, and he asks if I have ever heard of Judy Garland? Like she's this great discovery he's just made. So, of course, I say "yes." And he gets all excited and puts on the *Star is Born* soundtrack and begins singing along as he drives. Louder than Judy. Louder than anyone in the history of music. Right in my ear. And of course he can't sing. Not a note. So there I am, listening to "The Man that Got Away" sung off-tune by an Ex-Mormon at the top of his lungs. And he's the world's worst driver to boot, doing like 85 miles per hour. If he wasn't driving so fast, I would have rolled out of the car. I'm not sure he would have even noticed. And - *believe it or not* - the date went downhill from there. He took me to a cookout at his parents' house. *Who goes on a first date to their parents' house?* Both of whom are still very much Mormon. And not at all happy with their son's newly discovered lifestyle. Nor are they happy with me! He introduced me to them and they just glared at me. Like I personally killed Brigham Young. But wait, there's more! Turns out, all of the meat at this cookout - and who knew that Mormons eat meat? - All of the meat was *deer meat* from some Mormon hunting trip. *Deer meat.* We were eating Bambi. The only good part was that his mother made crème brûlée. It wasn't as good as yours of course, but at least the day wasn't a total bust. I told him I had to be at work the next day and asked if we could leave early. And he said, "But if we leave now, we won't be able to have sex." And I said, "Exactly." *(beat)* I swear, I'm going to have to start dating men my own age. You older guys are killing me.

---

Lawrence Harbison

# DEER

*Aaron Mark*

Seriocomic
Ken, fifties

*In the dead of night, Ken and Cynthia, whose mother's funeral they've just attended, are en route to their house in the Poconos for their first weekend alone together in twenty-five years. Cynthia drives, ignoring Ken as he chatters away.*

## KEN

You didn't start reading my manuscript yet, did you? Cynthia? Because you said you'd read it last week, that's what you said. And I don't want to be obnoxious, obviously you've been preoccupied with the funeral, but – If you'd read it this weekend, that would really be helpful, cause you did say you'd – Did I tell you what it's about? Because I don't want to give it away, but I'm anxious to – Well, I'll tell you: It's just a novella, it's inspired by that story, that thing that happened in Nebraska last year, you remember that? That woman, she's walking along, on the street, talking on a cell phone, and a guy on a motorcycle rides by and the noise is so loud – So violently, deafeningly loud – That the woman on the phone - Without thinking - She pulls out a handgun, like a, like a little handgun, she carries it around for protection, right, and she *shoots* the guy on the motorcycle! Just – As a reflex, a reaction to the noise, she shoots him! And then – Well, I shouldn't give away the rest, but that's what this new book is – The novella – A sort of fictionalization of that, the story of this woman who reacts this way to the noise, someone who seems perfectly normal, perfectly together, and she just snaps. And then how the people around her deal with it, after the fact, which is to say, well – Alright, I'll give it away: She got off! In real life – In Nebraska, you remember? She's a free woman, walking around with her concealed weapon! So she gets off. In the book. But it's more complicated than that, it always is. God, I really hate to give it away, but since you asked. Beat. But you'll read it this weekend, yes? Maybe after the kayaking? Cause you don't have anything else to do. Or tonight? You could read it tonight if you want, if you're that interested. You know…I've been doing the treadmill, Cynthia. Getting my stamina back. Feeling good, pretty good. And

I haven't masturbated in, maybe…a week? You know what that means… And I've been taking zinc. I feel like a young sprite. Like a frat boy, I swear to God. Like a horny Swedish frat boy. I don't know why "Swedish," why "Swedish"? I just said that, but I don't know what the reference is. Do they have frat boys in Scandinavia? You don't know, you've never been there. Anyway, I am ready to make love. To make *love*. To my *love*. Okay, I lied, I did masturbate, I masturbated yesterday, but only because I knew this was coming – Tonight – And I was fucking paranoid, you know, 'cause it's been so long, I didn't wanna be too, you know - For *you*. Just cause it's been so…So I did it for you, Cynthia. See? I'm always looking out for you.

For information on this author,
click on the WRITERS tab at www.smithandkraus.com.

# DINNER AT HOME BETWEEN DEATHS

_Andrea Lepcio_

Dramatic
Sean, forties-fifties

_Sean is speaking to Fiona directly. His sister-in-law, Kat, is also present. He has confessed he was sleeping with his employee, Lily, has been defrauding his investors for five years and has killed Lily after she found him out. He and Fiona are devout Catholics. He is desperate for Fiona to understand why he did what he has done. He still holds out hope she will stay with him and escape to homeland, Ireland._

## SEAN

I'll go to confession. I'll gladly go every day though I'll never be cleaned, you know that now, God forgive me, I'll never be clean again. I'm sick of it, Fee, my god, sick to death of... Caretaking everyone's hopes and dreams. Investors crying. Regulators braying. They look at the sky and see one color. Blue or grey. Oh, maybe they see a cloud coming in and think the worst. But that's all they can see. Blue good. Grey bad. Red sky at morning sailor take warning. Red sky at night sailor delight. But there I was alone seeing the sky for the mystery it is. Knowing that what happens tomorrow has nothing to do with what happened yesterday. That's what my model captured. Until it didn't. Until options and derivatives replaced the real. Till there was no real left. Only what could be imagined. Traded for the sake of trading. The regulators chasing their tails as if they could understand a fragment of what was taking place under their noses. The lot of them blind though the sky was there the whole time for them to see if only they could see.

# DRAW THE CIRCLE

*Mashuq Mushtaq Deen*

Dramatic
Matt, late twenties

*The protagonist, Shireen, has come out to friends and family about being transgender, and asked them to use male pronouns from now on. For Matt, who wants to be supportive, this is hard for him to do because Shireen looks the same, and he keeps messing up, and this embarrasses him*

## MATT

So we were all in Boston visiting Annie—it was me and my wife, Sara, Molly and Shireen, and we were all staying at Annie's place. And then Molly said they had something to tell us. We knew they weren't pregnant, so it was either a puppy, a wedding or a brain tumor? Not even close. My wife and Molly got into a huge fight, lasted hours. Sara was talking about the patriarchy and how they're all third-generation girl scouts—well, even their dad is a card-carrying member—and Sara went on about how "girls can do anything, any job, date anyone, be strong, you don't NEED a guy, and Shireen, she's a pretty masculine woman, and that's fine, that's strong, to be your own woman no matter what the world tells you, so why does she want to go and be a HE now?!" And Shireen said, "I feel more like a guy, so I want to be called HE." So we have to start calling Shireen HE. I try to do that. Molly kept saying, "he wants to be seen," but I see her and she still looks the same to me, she still looks like Shireen. And I wasn't the only one who was havin' a hard time saying HE, so she decided to change her name to DEEN to make it easier, but that was just another thing to remember. And I try to say SHE—I mean HE, fuck—well, it's hard to think about it every minute, sometimes I just want to have a fucking conversation without having to watch every word I say! And then, I felt stupid, like I couldn't get it and people would laugh, and it all felt made up anyway, like a game or something. She was still the same Shireen, I didn't see why we had to call her something different now!

# EMPATHITRAX

*Ana Nogueira*

Dramatic
Matty D, early thirties

*Empathitrax imagines a near future where a drug by the same name hits the market and allows people to feel what another person is feeling simply by touching them. In this monologue, Matty D talks to his best friend about how he is using the drug to better understand the women he dates. The only thing is, those women don't know he is under the influence.*

## MATTY D

Look, I just realized, I don't like to admit this, but I recently realized that for a long time I saw women as sort of empty. Or, no, not empty but like, as projections of me, right? Like -if I'm having a good time then I just assume that they must be having a good time. Or if I'm bored then so are they. But then I took this shit and I realized that they have like *so much* going on. And that I am usually dead wrong about what I assumed she was going through. Sure, *I* might be having a good time but it turns out that she's actually kind of nervous. So, okay. I can help calm her. Or when she's talking about her job that I think sounds like the most boring fucking thing on the planet, I touch her and realize that she's actually like, super passionate about it. Now I'm sorta passionate about it too! It's beautiful. You know, some people? They don't need the fucking drug. They just feel shit, they just get it. They can tune into another person like, instantly. It comes naturally to them. It doesn't come naturally to me, okay? And honestly, I think that's what has been getting in the way of me finding someone.

For information on this author,
click on the WRITERS tab at www.smithandkraus.com.

# EMPATHITRAX

## Ana Nogueira

Dramatic
Joe, early thirties

Empathitrax *imagines a near future where a drug by the same name hits the market and allows people to feel what another person is feeling simply by touching them. In this monologue Joe, an employee for the company that manufactures the drug, tries to convince a couple to go ahead and buy another round of pills. The couple has been struggling under the influence due to the woman's severe depression, and her partner wants to call it quits. Joe pushes him to reconsider even though the last round caused led to some unpleasant revelations within their relationship.*

### JOE

Many people who were previously medicated for various mental illnesses: generalized anxiety disorder, social anxiety, depression, seasonal depression, post-traumatic stress disorder, ADD, ADHD, body dismorphic disorder, obsessive compulsive disorder, bipolar I, bipolar II, and panic disorder, to name a few, choose to go off their medications to share with their partner what they call their "true selves." It can be very useful in those scenarios. Our users feel that the solidarity experienced when a previously isolating feeling is able to be shared not only lifts much of the burden and therefore the horror of their illness but also creates a deep closeness between them and their partner that transforms the sickness from a curse into a sort of a blessing. This is not a quick fix. Prolonged and regular use is key to achieving the desired goal of ultimate intimacy and understanding. I can put in another order for a box of six. We also have a frequent users program where you will get a recurring box every month / for a discounted price of … I assure, sir, this has been very affective for other users. It's extremely common for there to be resistance at first. We never claimed that the experience of using is consistently pleasant, but a lot can be gained in a relationship from a shared unpleasant and sometimes painful experiences. And remember: these feelings, like all feelings, are temporary. If you have had positive experiences under the influence in the past then it is safe to say that you will continue to have them in the future. A bump in the road like this merely signals progress. And for a couple as committed to one another as the two of you are, I have no doubt there are greener pastures just a little ways down the road. This is the woman who's brain you said you wanted to study. The one you are addicted to. I'm sure you still feel that way, after all these years. Shall I put in another order?

For information on this author,
click on the WRITERS tab at www.smithandkraus.com.

comes over me, suddenly. And I say to her: "Honey? *Honey.* Put down the dish. Come with me." And I bring her into the living room, and we laid down on the couch, and I laid my head on her stomach, and I said to her: "*All we can do now is wait.* And read. Let's just read *this one book.*" *(Remembers.)* "Let's pretend this is the only book in the world...." *(Remembers.)* And we opened this new book. And it was written by these two Hungarian women—from Budapest, I think—and right away we could tell that it was so... *different...* from all the other stuff we had read. Because they wrote about—about *respecting* your child.... And part of that respect, is, um.... *(Becoming emotional)* ... is... is not treating them like they're just a dumb *baby*, you know? Not just wiping their face when you think it's too dirty, not just shoving food into their mouth when you think they're hungry. Not, you know, not—*condescending* to them.... But instead, just... *telling* them what you're doing—*telling* your child... *(He begins to cry.)* "I'm going to wipe your face now, because you have chocolate on it. It's going to be uncomfortable, at first, because the wash cloth is going to be wet. But it's good for you. Here we go. " *(He cries.)* "I'm putting you in the bath. It's going to be warm. It might also be a bit startling, at first. But it will become pleasant, soon. Be patient. Trust me." *(He cries, harder.)* "I'm putting you in your crib. It's time to go to sleep. Sleep can be scary, because you have to be alone with your thoughts. But you're going to be okay. You are not alone. Mommy and I are right here with you. We love you so much. *(He sobs.) We love you...!* (He calms down a bit.) Goodnight." *(He stops crying; a beat.)* And stuff like that.

For information on this author,
click on the WRITERS tab at www.smithandkraus.com.

# HOUSE RULES

## *A. Rey Pamatmat*

Dramatic
Henry, early thirties', Filipino American

*Henry has broken up with his boyfriend Rod. Here, he tells him why. Ernie was Rod's father.*

### HENRY

Toto, Ernie's heart stopped, his brain, all of his organs failed. I was at the hospital every day, imagining you losing him. Imagining losing you. Wondering whether I was good enough to make all those decisions about his life or yours. And it wasn't enough to like the same movies, to tell you jokes that made you laugh, and to wake up next to you on a Wednesday morning, every morning for the rest of my life. It wasn't enough to be me. Suddenly, you needed a real boyfriend—fiancé. I haven't slept with a woman in ten years, and sometimes I still want to. I dream of living in Australia. I come home from work knowing if I could go back in time, I never would have become a doctor. I have no idea what I want, or who I am. So what if today I'm a good man, but tomorrow I fail, and next year I'm just a fucking horrible piece of shit? Your father was dying. That's not what you needed. You needed all of that out of your way. So I broke it off. I broke it off because I didn't want to hurt you or fail you or lose you forever.

# THE JAG

_Gino DiIorio_

Dramatic
Bone, forties

_Donald "Bone" Chicarella tries to be a wheeler dealer, but all his schemes seem destined to fail. He is speaking to Carla, trying to explain how he was always trying to win his father's love, but somehow it never worked out._

## BONE

The Jag? Ah, it's a shit box. Always breaking. Jaguars, everything on them is difficult. I was going to replace the heater core, right? Just to do that, I gotta take out the accelerator linkage for the carb, a valve cover, another temp sensor, and this isn't to do the repair, this is just to take it out so I can _get to_ the repair. You look at this car the wrong way, something falls off. See that's the thing, you love Jaguars. I used to marvel at them, you know? To them, it was like religion. When I was a kid, I'd look up at my old man and I could see up his nose, all the different colors, of the cars that he painted. Even though he wore a mask, it would seep through, and you could see it there, right on his face. Like a map of his day. And I thought he must have the worst job in the world. But he loved it. Both of them. A total wreck would come in, a twisted ball of metal, right? And they would circle it like a couple of prizefighters. They would speak in some kind of secret code and then all at once, they'd just attack it. Head would grab a dent puller and he'd slam that thing back till the car gave in to him. And Chick would be working the other side with a hammer and a toe dolly, and they'd be pulling it, jabbing it, grinding it, and before you know it, it was good as new. Better than new. They didn't fix anything. They improved it. To listen to them talk about grinding down the seat of a valve, as to so many thousandth's of an inch, so that the seat matched the top, the precision involved, to hear them talk about it…it was like a thing of beauty. But it was something….it was something I could never do.

# KENTUCKY

*Leah Nanako Winkler*

Dramatic
Adam, late twenties

*Adam talks to himself and the audience before attending a wedding rehearsal dinner with his high school crush.*

## ADAM

I miss how handsome I used to be. I miss how effortless everything seemed and was. I miss playing. And grabbing a rebound on the basketball court. The feeling of leather on my palms. And the sound of my name echoing in a gymnasium I miss enthusiasm. And desire. The feeling of desire. For the moment. For the future. For every girl I meet. I miss breakups not being such a big deal. I miss gliding through the hallways unaware of my own beauty as my limbs- they moved me effortlessly from classroom to classroom to practice to my car and I would drive it-the windows down while the air tussled my hair. And I would be *so handsome*. I mean, I'm not a bad looking guy now. Sure. But back then? Shit. Was I handsome! And now I miss it like I miss drinking alcohol without regret and going fast without consequence. And dancing hard unaware that there might not be a tomorrow. I miss my best friend D.J. who died of a heroin overdose. I miss not thinking. These days I'm thinking that I should have worked harder. Tried harder. Took better care of my hair I hope it doesn't thin like my father's will Gee I hope my belly doesn't swell. Darn. I hope , I hope. I hope=I hope I hope won't have to spend so many more nights alone listening to Jewel and Joni Mitchell while staring at the stars up above and wishing and wishing and wishing for love!

# THE KID CULT COSMOLOGY

## Graham Techler

Seriocomic
T.J., twelve (though played by an adult actor)

*T.J. is an awkward, lonely, obsessive middle school boy who—after witnessing what he believes to be a UFO with his friends Robby and Aaron—forms a three-person space cult in order to worship their (made up) alien god. At a sleepover, as the others fall asleep, T.J. ruminates on his inspiration for the cult idea.*

### T.J.

I read something online about this guy Claude. I forget his last name. It sounds kinda like Vacuum. But it's not. I'd never heard of him. Have you? Well, he's French. And he did all kinds of cool stuff. He was like a child pop star, and a sports journalist, and a racecar driver. But then apparently one day he was in a volcanic crater, just hanging out. And a ship came down from the sky. Just like with us. And the being in the ship told him all about how humans came to Earth, how other beings made humans and send messengers to teach them to be peaceful and stuff. And they said it was his job to spread this message to everyone. So he totally did, just like us. And he changed his name to something cool. He started telling people his story and they helped him to prepare for the aliens return. And once they also came back- the aliens- and took him up on their ship to another planet where he met Jesus and Buddha and guys like that. Then they taught him all about the mysteries of the universe. And because it was Jesus and Buddha and everybody they were like really good at it and he totally *got* everything. He just *got it*. He didn't have to think about it anymore. He totally *got it*. And now he's got like sixty-thousand people who believe him. And maybe they get it just like he does, but maybe they don't because he got abducted and everything but they're probably trying. Sixty-thousand is like sixty times everyone in the school. And he's got all these people all over the world who believe him and they're all on the same page, and even when they're not all together and he's not with those people he at least knows that there are people out there who get it like he gets it. I can't imagine Claude Vacuum ever feels lonely. And he gets to drive race cars.

# KILLING WOMEN

_Marisa Wegrzyn_

Seriocomic
Ramone, fifties

_Ramone, who runs a company of professional assassins, tells Abby how and why he hired her._

## RAMONE

I'm sorry you were offended. Abbs, you were a different woman before I got a hold of you. Now I'm sorry it came down to me taking action here, terminating your pet project. I know you're angry about a lot. Wyatt still needs your car. Gwen is dead. I don't expect you to like me, but I'm the boss, and I need you to—at the very least—respect that. Your first kill changes you. My first kill changed me. Immediately after I hired you, I did my research. I had to find out about you. I had to find who you loved. We got to talking about the women in our lives, during our game of cards, and you were his Angel. He was trying to win a pretty penny on the straight flush he had, said he wanted to buy you just the right engagement ring. Something nice, but not too flashy because he knew you wouldn't like that. You didn't know that? I thought you knew that. His hand went to the Jack and mine went to the King. It was a pretty wild bet. High stakes. The pilot lost big. The flight attendant and the pilot. Must've been romantic for you two. Flings in Paris, flings in Rome, wherever you wanted to go. He told me you'd watch Casablanca with him even though he knew you didn't like it. Because no matter how many times you watched it, the ending wouldn't change. _(Pause)_ That was your test Abby. If you could kill the man you loved, you could kill for me.

# LADIES DAY

*Alana Valentine*

Dramatic
Liam, twenty-five to thirty

*Liam is a gay man living in Broome, a remote part of Western Australia. He is speaking to Lorena, a playwright who has travelled to Broome to investigate the experiences of gay men living there. Lorena has been trying to build trust with Liam so that he will speak honestly about his experience.*

## LIAM

I met a guy at work the other day and his son's gay. And the way he spoke about his son was shocking. Like he's quite high in business and he was like, 'Yeah, one of my son's is a faggot and we don't get on because he lives in that gay world.' And I didn't come out to him at all but it really shocked me because I was like, 'Wow, that's your version of tolerance, huh? And that's your own son.' 'Yeah, we're not very close he's one of those gays.' One of those gays? There's a two way thing to it. During the wet season, when it's quiet, there's about five people on Grindr or something…but during the dry season when the backpackers hit town there's like seventy. So if you mean that sort of scene that's one thing. But there are a lot of gay people in town who don't want to be part of that but want to be part of a community. And people have been starting to talk about wanting to do something to acknowledge and celebrate that community. So we're going to start an organization called Pink Broome next year. To address issues, social justice stuff. I think Broome wants to be seen to be welcoming. I think we'll get money out of the council because it's about tourism. Broome is apparently going through a bit of a low economically so they're all convinced that the pink dollar will bring the money in. So I would imagine most people will be supportive and from what we've received feedback most people will be fine. And we will out the ones that don't. So to speak. Retailers will mostly be supportive, there's always an element that won't be supportive and that's…life.

For information on this author,
click on the WRITERS tab at www.smithandkraus.com.

# THE LEGEND OF GEORGIA MCBRIDE

*Matthew Lopez*

Dramatic
Rexy, twenties-thirties

*"Rexy" is short for Anorexia Nervosa, drag queen. She tells Casey, a
straight guy doing drag in secret, how and why she became a drag queen.*

## REXY

You ever been to Houston? Miserable town for a little gay boy to come
up in. Only place in the world I felt safe was inside a bar called the
Montrose Mining Company. That's where I put my first face on. So
this one night between shows, I walk out to my car to get my cigarettes
when a brick materializes out of nowhere and hits me in the face out
of nowhere and hits me in the face.

*(pointing to the scar)*

Right here. Then another brick hits me in the back of the head.

*(pointing to the back of her head)*

Right here. By now, I'm on the ground and I look up to see two of
Houston's most promising young citizens preparing to kick the living
shit out of me. I get to my feet, I face my attackers and I say "well,
motherfuckers: show me what you got." They did, all right.

*(pointing to the scar)*

Seven stitches.

*(pointing to the back of her head)*

Eighteen.

*(pointing to her nose)*

Broken.

*(pointing to her lip)*

Busted.

*(pointing to her teeth)*

False. I was sixteen years old. And I still have the guts to walk out
to my car every night as I am, even in this shitty, homophobic town.

Because I'm a drag queen, bitch. Drag ain't a hobby, baby. Drag ain't a night job. Drag is a protest. Drag is a raised fist inside a sequined glove. Drag is a lot of things, baby, but drag is not for sissies.

For information on this author,
click on the WRITERS tab at www.smithandkraus.com.

# LIFE SUCKS

*Aaron Posner*

Comic
Vanya, forty-five

*LIFE SUCKS is a hilarious loose adaptation of Chekhov's UNCLE VANYA. Vanya manages the estate of a professor who is rarely there. Here, he tells a visitor, Dr. Aster, what he thinks of the professor.*

## VANYA

I can't believe I used to think he was *brilliant*. I'd sit at his knee, practically, and just listen to him drone on and on and on about art and music and, you know, Buddhism and Symbolism and Veganism and any other -ism he was into at any given time, and I read all the books he told me to read until I realized he was utterly full of shit, that he only really understood about a fifth of everything he talked about and that— I mean, fuck, I can hurl nine dollar words around, too, you know… Why, I could profess it is not calumny, but rather axiomatic to aver that he's a scrofulous, vapid, orotund ass with inchoate, noisome notions, and a penchant for sesquipedalian elocution. Or I could just call him a pedantic prick and be done with it. The truth is I have ten times as much imagination and insight and and and… *understanding of the fucking universe* as he does, and yes, okay, yes, if Ella could see past my *tie* and my… *nerdy wimpishness* and my… *whatever*, and just see me for who I *really am*— and who he really is!— than she'd pack her bags, catch the first bus out of dodge, and show up on my door step!

# LIFE SUCKS

*Aaron Posner*

Comic
Vanya, forty-five

*LIFE SUCKS is a hilarious loose adaptation of Chekhov's UNCLE VANYA. Vanya manages the estate of a professor who is rarely there. Here, he tells a visitor, Dr. Aster, and others in the household what he thinks of the professor.*

## VANYA

You know what he teaches? You know what his *specialty* is in his rarified little enclave of academic elitism and self-aggrandizement? Semiotics. Semiotics! Signs! Symbols! Clues! It's the study of *clues*!!! I mean... *why*? Who gives a fuck? I have a sign for him: STOP! Stop "studying" things that no real person in the real world could ever *imagine* caring about! At least esoteric sciences can lead to... you know... new kinds of *wheat* or or or or or better drugs or windmills or whatever, but Christ On A Cracker, endless impassioned arguments about— look, I stole this article he wrote from his room to try to get some... here... here... "Semiotic Phenomenology & The Relational Constitution of Presence" HELLO?!?!? Oh, and wait, there's a subtitle, thank God, this will really clear things up: "Thematizing the Problematic through Human Speech Praxis " I mean... WHAT THE FUCK DOES THAT EVEN MEAN?!?! It's a vast conspiracy that costs real people gazillions of dollars each year. *Academics*! Privileged, arrogant fuckers arguing endlessly about esoteric minutiae so *stunningly meaningless* and *rampantly unimportant* that even they could not possibly care themselves, except that if they ever told anyone how little they cared they couldn't continue the absurd conspiracy of getting generations of over-privileged eighteen-year-old sparrow-farts to pay them and praise them and give them tenure and spend their time and our money arguing endlessly about... "The Phenomenology of Whatever-The-Fuck" and giving each other awards and making the rest of us feel like uncultured boobs and morons because we don't give a shit!

# LIFE SUCKS

## Aaron Posner

Seriocomic
Vanya, forty-five

*LIFE SUCKS is a hilarious adaptation of Chekhov's UNCLE VANYA. Here, Vanya, speaking to Ella, has realized the pointlessness of his life.*

### VANYA

Oh my God. *Nothing.* That's your answer. Not a thing. You're absolutely right. *This* is the "real me". This is it. This is all there is. This is me. And if I were you... I wouldn't be interested in me either. I swear to God it all just hit me. Just *now*. For the first time... I think my whole life I've been saying to myself—not just about you, but all the way back as far as this kind of thing goes. I've always thought "she" would choose me if only she really *knew me*. If she understood me. If only she knew what I'm really like, what I'm like deep down inside. How I mean so well. How much I want to do the right thing. How good my heart is. How much I hurt. How confused and lost I am... How hopeful... And maybe those are even true, maybe... But those are no more the "real me" than the lonely, whining, dissatisfied, pathetic *putz* who pesters you constantly with his inconvenient love. I swear I've always thought that the internal me was the "real me" and this guy—the one in the world, the one just "doing things" was... I don't know... a facsimile. Not important. Just "the guy out there doing things"... But now... I mean, Jesus, if I'm *that* guy, that *external* guy— just the sum total of the shit I *do*— then Christ, I just want to scrape out what left of my heart with a grapefruit spoon... Because it's what you DO that matters, right? That's actually what I've always liked best about Jewish theology. No sinning in your heart. No being punished for your thoughts. It's actions! Not what you say, or think, or *feel*, but what you DO. And if the real me is this guy, this *schmuck* who just wanders through the world bothering people... Then I am so royally fucked I don't what to do.

# LOST IN LIMBO

*Nicholas Priore*

Dramatic
Apollo, twenty-four

*Apollo has awakened from a dream and is recording some of what he has just experienced.*

## APOLLO

I finally figured it out! Wait...no, fuck, where'd it go? Every time I have an epiphany, it wakes me up and then leaves in the next moment, leaving behind only it's warm afterglow...what wonderful dream was this? I can hardly remember. But it was perfection, perhaps something that cannot survive in the real world...and so it comes in that nebulous state between sleeping and waking, just about to slip into dream logic or about to lift out of it...in this transitional state, The cosmos reveals itself to me, the universe in all its complexity narrowed into a single moment of crystalline divinity. Maybe it's the voice of God, which would explode my conscious mind, and so it can only speak to my subconscious. What cruel trick is this, that I am only allowed a glimpse and must spend the rest of my day trying to retain what had come and gone so fast...I get closer and closer each time, snatching at it, but never quite catching it...my any attempt to bring it with me can only be an inferior adaptation by the best of my ability. All I can remember of this recurring dream is that I am sifting for gold in a stream, when suddenly I see in the water something more beautiful than my insufficient language can describe, and for the sake of becoming tangible in my hands, it manifests into a perfect golden nugget. And there it is. In my hands. Absolute truth, with a wholeness and totality that is beyond my comprehension. I can look all I want, but once I try to close it in my palm, I awaken to the sad realization that I had not carried it with me. I hope one day it returns to stay, allows me to make it known to the world in all its glory. The greatest gift one can only dream of...a gift that can only be felt and never verbalized, for to verbalize it would be to bastardize something we can never understand...but still I try...

# LULLABY

*Michael Elyanow*

Dramatic
Gabriel, fifties

*Gabriel has been having an argument with his daughter, who has been pushing him to stop enabling her alcoholic mother (his wife). Upset, he tells Cassie the reason why he'll never give up on the woman he married.*

## GABRIEL

Let me tell you something about your mother. You didn't know her before. What she did for me. How she brought me out, opened me up. The guys on campus, they were all sick with envy—how did a shmuck like me get her? God knows she wasn't perfect, she was difficult and argumentative, but adventurous and smart, too. So goddamn smart I didn't understand half the things she was saying at first. I spent my nights in the library just catching up so I could maintain conversation. You fall in love with somebody like that, you're IN IT for the rest. You make a vow, for better or worse, and whatever that worse is, you'll take it. ...Your mother is a warm and lovely woman with a disease. She is a masterful journalist with a disease. She has three books and dozens of published articles behind her and she has a disease. I have watched your mother's disease eat her alive, tearing her brilliance apart bit by bit, skin and hair and memory. You think it's not painful? That I don't feel gypped? Of course, I do. The whole thing is a goddamn tragedy unparalleled.

# MAGIC TRICK

## *Mariah MacCarthy*

Comic
Eric, mid-thirties

*Eric's paraplegic girlfriend, Bana, has disappeared from their apartment overnight—along with all her belongings. He's decided to track down the last person they saw together, a burlesque dancer named Clara, to try to figure out what happened. He and Clara have gotten drunk together, and now he's trying to get her to go home with him.*

### ERIC

Y'know who're great lovers? The grieving. Honestly. Let me tell you something. My dad died when I was 25, and my family's Orthodox Jewish so I sat shiva for him. OK, so I had this girlfriend at the time, and I had to sit shiva and she said, "I think we're gonna have great sex when you're done sitting shiva," and I said, "I think you're right." And so that night, after I was done, I went over there and she just came to the door and...how do I put this...She came eight times. Eight. And I know there are those girls that can just do that, where that's, like, Tuesday for them, but Jenna was not one of those girls. I came four, which Bana would tell you if she were here is highly unusual for me, but that's neither here nor there. The point is. Happy, sad, whatever, I am a fantastic lover. But when I'm grieving—which I most certainly am right now, in case you couldn't tell—I'm a golden god, Clara. I don't even have to exaggerate. I am just that good. *(Beat)* Tell you what. I'm gonna go use the little boys' room. If you're gone when I get back, I'll understand, no hard feelings. If you're here...both of us will probably have a very pleasant night.

# *A MOON FOR THE MISBEGOTTEN* AT THE CHARLES-VILLE SUMMER THEATRE FESTIVAL

*Graham Techler*

Comic
Mr. Engleton, seventy

*Mr. Engleton is a wealthy Northeastern man in his 70s who, like many wealthy Northeastern men in their 70s, likes to consider himself a patron of the arts. However, when he pushes a disgruntled intern at the Charles-ville Summer Theatre Festival a bit too far, he finds himself in a literal/ physical/verbal/magical duel with her. Here, he delivers his final blow.*

## MR. ENGLETON

Now listen here. I worked for forty years. Forty years owning a chain of seafood take-out restaurants my father built with his own two hands. You think I care about seafood? I don't care a wink about seafood and I never did. If I never see another shrimp again it will be too soon. That was the best part about it being a take-out place; no matter where you took your meal it was at least out of my sight. Not that I spent much time at an actual Captain's Cove location. Oh no. I spent the bulk of my time on the front lines. In the corporate office. Doing the grunt work most fry cooks would shudder to think of. Placing new locations around the Northeast. Making public statements when that dumb kid ate a lobster that was still alive. It was a nightmare. You think I care about lobsters? You think wrong. Let me paint a picture for you. You've lived your life on a foundation of fish sticks. At the end of the road you make your son the CEO and scoot for a life of leisure with your beautiful wife. You dream of sailing around the world. Owning a minor league baseball team. But it turns out people don't love seafood like they used to. Turns out you're just "buy your granddaughter a Maserati for her sweet sixteen" rich and not "secede from the U.S. on a private island" rich. So you think back to your father. What would he want? He was a man of great passion and artistic temperament. The record player always hummed a line of Puccini in his office in the early days of Captain's Cove. He would want you to use this disposable income to make the world a more beautiful place. Then you see that Jim Parsons from TV is going to be in a play at Charlesville and your wife wants to see him so that's that. You make a donation so you can feel a part of something bigger. You now know that the world of art simply cannot turn without you pushing it! And when you walk into the theatre you want all these little roaches to know it! It is by your hand that you have a theatre at all! And you want a little respect. And you goddamn want to see your name in the "Lighting Designer's Circle" section of the lord loving program!

# THE MORNING AFTER GRACE

*Carey Crim*

Dramatic
Ollie, sixty-nine

*Abigail, a grief counselor, has urged Ollie, a former Major League base-ball player, to tell his 92 year-old father that he's gay. This is a trial run.*

## OLLIE

When I was fourteen... I was hanging out one Saturday in the back yard with my friend Jeff Mack. He had moved and I hadn't seen him since Little League so we were catching up. You and mom were out. I don't remember where. The hardware store I think. You never could go anywhere alone. I remember that he was telling me about his new school and some girl there. But all I could see were his lips. How they moved. How soft they looked. And I'm not exactly sure when, but somehow, he had moved his face a little closer and I had moved my face a little closer and before I knew it, our lips were almost touching and he wasn't pulling back and I wasn't pulling back and then... our lips were actually touching. And neither of us could breathe or move. That was my first kiss. And it was the most real and alive I had ever felt. The next thing I felt was your hand slamming into the back of my head. You yelled at Jeff to go home and you dragged me into the house. You had never hit any of us kids before. But that afternoon, you used your belt and you used it hard. You made it clear, if I continued down that path, I would not be welcome. By you. By my team. By anyone that mattered to me. I'm not entirely blaming you. The world was different then. You did what a lot of fathers did. And some still do. But I'm telling you now. If you want to come and live with me, you'll be living with two men, two men who love each other more than they ever thought possible. You'll be getting to know your son. All of me. Because I won't hide it anymore. Not from you. Not from myself. Not from anyone. It took fifty-five years, but I am done hiding. Dad, I'm gay.

For information on this author,
click on the WRITERS tab at www.smithandkraus.com.

# MR. JOY

*Daniel Beaty*

Seriocomic
DeShawn, sixteen

*DeShawn is a sixteen year-old energetic, charismatic young black man
who lives in Harlem. He is speaking to one of his friends.*

## DeSHAWN

Dre! Yo!!! What up man?! When you get home? Yo' moms was saying she was hoping you get out this week, but— Look at you, looking
all swole, *(He flexes his muscles.)* Looking all buff like the Rock but
chocolate. Yo', you get my letters man? Why you ain't let me come
visit? Shoot, we ain't got to talk about it, I'm just glad you home. You
like my shoes? I see you checking them out. Mr. Joy just polished
them up for me. Yeah that old man still there—you know those Chinese
live a long time. Yeah, he still wearin' that same outfit— Black shoes,
gray pants—exactly I was like yo', Mr. Joy, you need to get to Target
or something— Yo! You home from prison on the same day I'm spit-
tin' my poem at church. That's God man! Ah, come on, Dre, don't
start—I ain't no church boy, I still gots my swag. I started going when
you got locked up. You should come with me? No, there ain't no two
drink minimum—it's church! It's safe, I promise—ain't no crazy white
boy gone shoot up my church— Too many people from the hood; he
wouldn't be the only one packing. You know, it ain't even safe to sit out
here and chill in these projects anymore. You hear about what happened
to JaQuarius last night? JaQuarius was just sitting here, chillin', You
know, checking out the sights—lookin' at the hunnies, When some
guys from one of these gangs walk by with they girls. And one of the
guys, he catches JaQuarius checking out his girl, And the guy is like,
"Yo', why you disrespecting me, son? Stop staring at my girl!" And
JaQuarius is like, "No disrespect man." But the guy, he won't let it
go, Next thing you know, the guy and his boys take JaQuarius up to
the roof, They beat him, then they throw him off the 36$^{th}$ floor. And you
know what, Dre, it wasn't in the news or nothing. Rich folks movin' in
our hood everyday – whites, blacks, Asians, Buying these million dollar
condos and brownstones— And we out here dyin' and nobody's talking
about it Not even black folks— So you gone come check me out? I

know church ain't yo' thing— But Dre, it's like…it's like I'm getting to know God like for real— Like He be talking to me and stuff— No, I can't get you the numbers to the lotto. I ain't talkin' about no physic Ms. Cleo stuff, I'm just talkin' about like basic stuff like about my life. Check it, my Pastor, he always be talking about faith, And if you ask God for something like to keep yo' family safe or whatever, You have to have Faith and believe He gone do it. 'Cause He's our Father and He loves us. But that's like really hard for me, 'Cause you know like both of us,  Both of our fathers are in prison and we ain't really know 'em, But then one night I'm lying in my bed,  And I hear this voice, and it's like, "DeShawn," And I turn on the lights but nobody's here, And then I hear it again, "DeShawn,"And I'm thinking my mind is playing tricks on me, So I get real quiet and I hear, "DeShawn, this is your Heavenly Father, You can't have a relationship with me, your Heavenly Father Like I was your natural father who abandoned you and didn't keep his word. I will not leave you. Have faith and I will show you what it means to truly have a father." Deep right? And you know, after that, I was like bet, let me give this Faith thing a try, And my moms, my grandmoms, they safe  And I'm okay, and you made it back safe, lookin' all buff like Conan the Negro Man— Yo' Dre man, I'm really glad you home.

# NO SISTERS
## *Aaron Posner*

Seriocomic
Solyony, thirties

*In this brilliant goof on Chekhov's THE SISTERS, Solyony is even more of a misanthrope than he was in the original, and he has a lot to say about the state of the world. Here, he is with a group of other characters, but much of this is direct address to the audience.*

### SOL

*(To a particular person in the audience... a person he picks out deliberately with some sense of selection by look or energy or...)*

You, sir/ma'am/fella. You're stupid, right? Right? You do stupid things. You've made some stupid choices, done stupid things you regret, things you would never want to admit to in front of this crowd, because they were so...... *stupid.* Am I right? And the rest of you? How many of you are stupid? How many of you do stupid things on a regular basis? I see you. Liars. You're all cringing slightly (or hugely) inside right now, aren't you, because I might call on you next and you might be forced, if only facially, to admit that you, too, are among the ranks of The Stupid, or... in other words... The Human. Human equals stupid. Right? Right??? I mean—look at the world right now. RIGHT NOW! The insane shit that is flying around the airwaves. You see it right? They won! Did you not notice? They did! Them! The Forces! The current level of stupidity and horror can't be real except for the fucking... unfathomable fact that it totally is! Everywhere. You watch the news... and the fake news... and you can't separate the parodies from the reality because, you know, it has finally, finally, finally worked! We're finally are SO FUCKING CONFUSED by making the news sound like entertainment and entertainment mimic the news, and newspapers sounding like tabloids and "reality" shows being faker than fictional shows that are actually realer to us than our own lives that we are all fucking caught up and confused and docile as fucking sheep so we can led wherever The Forces want us to go. The Forces of MONEY! The Forces of Power! The Forces want to keep them up and us down, them selling and us buying whatever the FUCK they want to sell us! What other Forces have there ever been ever anywhere?

# NO SISTERS

*Aaron Posner*

Seriocomic
Solyony, thirties

*NO SISTERS in a wild goof on Chekhov's THREE SISTERS. Here, the misanthropic Solyony tells Tuzenbach about a weird dream he had.*

### SOL

Yeah, so... In this... In this dream I was having... try-outs or some-thing for this Chekhov play, I don't know which one, at least I think they were the try-outs, but I was never quite clear who was coming or why or what exactly the play was or who the characters were or what exactly my relationship to any or all of the people who were auditioning was... or could be... or should be... So, in the dream it was a dark and stormy morning... and the wind was really blowing around the rain and the trees and I heard yelling outside and I went into a kind of terrace greenhouse kind of room on the second floor, near where I was having these try-outs or whatever and I realize the yelling is coming from a tree and someone is high up in the air holding onto a tree branch for dear life while he is just whipping through the air and the rain and flailing all about and just yelling his head off so I start running about trying to think how I can help, can I get him a a a rope or a a a a mattress to land on, and I suddenly peer closer at him as he's just ...

*(Impersonates a body being whipped around in a hurricane.)*

... and realize... or I think I realize... that the poor schmuck being flung around by a tree in a storm... is me. Me. I'm out there on this tree branch terrified, yelling and making such a ruckus that I am dis-turbing my own try-outs for a Chekhov play... I'm not sure which one... or who's auditioning... or why we're having the auditions on this dark and stormy morning, or... and I'm also inside seeing all this. I am both places at the same time and totally confused by the whole thing. So, what do you think it means?

# OD

*Nicholas Priore*

Dramatic
Nick Jr, late twenties

*Nick Jr. has been trying to explain to his hospital sitter that his overdose was just for fun and not a suicide attempt so that she will let him go, but his patience has now worn thin.*

## NICK JR

NO! I tried keepin my cool cuz I know you'd love any reason to transfer me to the psyche ward, but fuck this and fuck you. ALL OF YOU! You just keep people waitin', that's all you do. My father died here, you let him slip away…brain aneurism, you people had him waiting in a room like this, the man was blind, how do you think that musta felt, all the sudden you're blind in a room waiting for a cat scan, which was too little too late by the time you got him in there, a second hemorrhage more devastating than the first, the knockout punch…you let him sit there and wonder why the fuck he couldn't see anything, how scared must he have been? How come you had to wait for the aftershock to hit before you did anything? Fuck, drill a hole in his head, let that blood out, do somethin', get medieval if you have to, anything but fuckin nothing! There was a window of time, maybe just a moment, when he coulda been saved, and you missed it. This place is a piece'a shit and you should all be ashamed. (His anger melts into sadness and defeat) I have these dreams where he's dying, like he doesn't seem sick at all but there is an unspoken understanding that he's dying. I've had this dream a number of times in the past year … and every time we just go about our business, ignoring the ugly stinking elephant in the room…sometimes it occurs to me that I should ask, maybe, "How ya feelin', Dad?" or "Has anything changed?" or maybe even start to say goodbye…and then I stop. And I say nothing. There's a sense of hope in that silence…like if we just don't say it, then the inevitable will stay at bay. Dream logic I guess, but it keeps us from ever mentioning anything about it…not a single word. Few times, I built up the nerve to breathe in a breath of inquiry…and then I wake up, and exhale a breath of relief that it was only a dream…and then I remember, he's already gone. But then, and this is the fucked up part, after a moment or so of

---

grief, I feel relief again. Relief that it's all behind me. In the dream I'm anticipating the unthinkable, trying to wrap my head around it… and when I wake up, the grief is still there, but the dread is gone. Not sure which is worse. When somethin' so sudden leads to somethin' so final, it just doesn't register. I'm not sayin' I wish he died a long painful death…of course I'm glad he never suffered…hope not. And I'm not sayin' it's any easier for the family that way…I can't imagine watching a loved one slowly deteriorate over time, I get to skip over that part every time I wake up. I'm just sayin' that when it all happens inside a single fucking morning, you don't get to say or do the things you might have had time for if you knew for a while. If someone's sick, there's time, though never enough I'm sure, to try and digest the unimaginable before it becomes a part of reality. We had no time for that…it was a fuckin' sucker punch. In my dreams, I have that time I never had in real life…to talk about it with him, say what I need to say, come to some sort of terms while he's still there in front of me. That is a gift…a gift I for which I am very grateful…but still I reject it night after night. Even in my dreams, I embrace the hope that lies only in denial…one day we'll talk about it…when we're ready. Maybe then I can say goodbye. Maybe then I can cry.

For information on this author,
click on the WRITERS tab at www.smithandkraus.com.

# ON CLOVER ROAD

*Steven Dietz*

Dramatic
Stine, fifties

*Stine is a professional de-programmer, hired by the mother of a teenaged girl who has been lured into a cult. He has her locked in the bathroom of a motel as he confronts her with the truth.*

### STINE

What Brody-Boy - or I guess the screen name was actually "Brody-Boy-69" - what this boy wanted from you wasn't *cute at all*, was it Jessie? This *BOY* was in fact a forty-two year-old man living in his mother's basement who found you online and started texting you on your new phone - *the phone your mom bought to keep you SAFE FROM PEOPLE LIKE THAT —- and see the thing is: I've read those texts - just like your mom did - and it's clear to me that "Brody-Boy- 69" had plans for you, honey.* Sure, he'd have to get past that first meeting - they all know that, these scumbags - they know there will be that moment when you see that "Brody-Boy" is not a sweet sixteen year old kid with long hair and nice eyes who plays guitar *and thinks you are the prettiest thing God ever put on this Earth.* No, this forty-two year-old convicted sex offender - with herpes and homemade tattoos and the given name of Brian Patrick Anderson - he's gonna have to get you past that awkward first moment when you show up in your tight jeans and your cute little top - only to find out you've been *duped.* But you know what, Jessie? - *guys like that find a way* —OH, YEAH, THEY ALWAYS FIND A WAY —- and of course the RUSH YOU'RE GONNA FEEL in keeping a secret from your Mom - "let's not tell her, okay?" - "let's just keep it between us" - "cause it's cool, we're cool, right?" - *and that's how forty-two year-old drifters get their hands down the pants of stupid little girls like you.*

# ONEGIN AND TATYANA IN ODESSA

## Don Nigro

Seriocomic
Onegin, late twenties

*In this play based on Alexander Pushkin's long poem Eugene Onegin, Onegin and his younger friend Lensky are riding home in a carriage in the dark after their first visit to their country neighbors, the Larins. Lensky has wanted to show Onegin his beloved Olga, but Onegin is much more interested in her smart, silent, moody sister Tatyana. Here Lensky, sitting beside Onegin in the carriage, has just asked him what he thought of Olga, expecting Onegin to go into rhapsodies about her beauty. Onegin realizes in the middle of his critique of Olga that he's hurt Lensky's feelings. He is not used to dealing with people so innocent and tender-hearted, and tries, with some difficulty, to apologize, explain himself, and communicate to Lensky that he actually does very much value his friendship. The reference to Pushkin as imaginary is a joke between them, since Onegin is always talking about Pushkin but we never see him.*

## ONEGIN

Olga is attractive enough, in an ordinary sort of way. But if I was a romantic young fellow who recites Byron at the drop of a hat, I'd have gone after the other one. Olga's got a pretty face, but, chess triumphs notwithstanding, her head's as empty as the inside of a balloon. But that other one—a man can't help wondering what's going on underneath. Was that a rat? We've run over a rat. It moved like a rat. Where the hell is he taking us? Budapest? What? Now you've gone quiet. Have I offended you? I haven't sufficiently worshipped at the feet of your goddess? You'll have to make allowances for me. Being the Devil's stepchild, I am compulsively drawn to darkness, and my life has been a series of interrupted digressions and frantic copulations on Oriental rugs with other men's wives. I've grown jaded and exhausted by a series of bewildering and apparently endless betrayals. And I'm fickle by nature. Nothing in my world lasts, except winter, which seems to go on forever. In Russia our summers go by in the blink of an eye, so we spend them frantically drowning ourselves in erotic misery. I move disconsolately from one absurd puppet show to the next. I have abandoned so many. I've given up chasing women. They're so easy to catch, there's no real sport in it. And I thought, well, I'm a born liar,

I should write, like my imaginary friend Pushkin, but when I actually took the trouble to look inside myself I discovered there was nothing there. I try to read. It's all meaningless. I sit among ticking clocks and rows of books like tombstones. So when you showed up—someone with at least half a brain that I could talk to, whose company I surprised myself by actually looking forward to—I'm just learning the art of friendship, rather late in the game. Be patient with me, and in turn I'll try and teach you something about life, even though you will undoubtedly do exactly the opposite of what I tell you. I would never purposely offend you. I don't know how to be anybody's friend, really.

## ONEGIN AND TATYANA IN ODESSA
## Don Nigro

Dramatic
Onegin, late twenties

*Eugene Onegin, hero of the great Alexander Pushkin poem upon which this play is based, has inherited a rich uncle's estate in the country, where he is very bored and lonely until his young friend Lensky talks him into visiting their neighbor, the widow Larin and her two beautiful daughters. The elder daughter, Tatyana, very smart but also very young and inexperienced, has never met anyone like the dashing Onegin, falls instantly in love with him, and has sent him a passionate letter offering herself to him. Onegin is used to the jaded, sophisticated society of St Petersburg, where everybody sleeps with everybody, sex is a game, and love a joke. He is quite troubled by the letter he's just read and not at all sure how to react. Her innocence and vulnerability, combined with her intelligence and passion, are not at all within the range of his previous experience. Here he is talking to himself, trying to figure out how to handle this situation, and the unusual and uncomfortable feelings it has aroused in him.*

ONEGIN

She is so innocent. Well, she seems innocent. But no woman is innocent. It's an insult to a woman's intelligence to think of her as innocent. She knows. Maybe she doesn't know that she knows. Or doesn't want to admit to others or to herself that she knows. But in her heart, she knows that she's an animal like me. And something else. What it is, I don't know. Or maybe I know, but I don't want to know that I know, either. I need a drink. I need many drinks. It's a dangerous person who feels things so deeply. I myself much prefer skimming upon the surface like a dragon fly. I understand a woman who's calculating, selfish and fickle. But girls like this one, who appear to be something else, are much more dangerous. She loves unconditionally, like a child. She doesn't know how to play the game. She's a danger to herself and to everyone who gets near her. I don't understand these people. Everything is written in another language, but translation is hopeless. I have no code book. It is all hieroglyphics. I stopped translating Vergil when he got to Hell, and I've been there ever since. All love is deception. Either deception of the beloved or deception of one's self, or both. All lovers are delusional. Tatyana looks at the moon, writing a letter by moonlight, leaning on her elbows. Her nightgown slips down from her shoulder. She takes no notice of the sunrise. We spend our whole lives writing the same letter over and over again. But who is the letter for? Somebody in our heads. Poor Tatyana. I will now shed tears with you. You have offered yourself up naked to a monster. Not me. Love is the monstrous thing, waiting at the center of the labyrinth to devour you. She sits in the garden in the dark and broods, and the moon looks down upon her, as I do. And the moon has no pity.

# OTHER THAN HONORABLE
## Jamie Pachino

Dramatic
Gideon, Army Brigadier General, late forties

*Brigadier General Gideon Kane, early forties, a career army man, now up for the position of Deputy Inspector General of the Army. Here, Gideon speaks to Grace Rattigan, a former officer under his supervision, with whom he had an affair— and then violently sexually assaulted when she tried to end their relationship. It's been 8 years since that assault, and Grace is now an attorney leading a case against Gideon for sexually based crimes that have occurred on the base where he was Commander.*

### GIDEON

You were the love of my life. …You just came too late. I had a career to protect then, a wife who only stood by me even after we couldn't have children. If I divorced her and it came out we'd had an affair, it would have ended my career, disgraced her, and what would we have had? I realize you were a casualty, I see now how much it affected you. I shouldn't have gotten involved in the first place, but you were a spectacular girl. Still are. Look at you. Maybe I never apologized properly, and for that I'm sorry. I'm sorry I didn't pick you. I guess that hurt more than I imagined. But maybe now I've admitted I could have handled things better, we can be realistic about what's going on here. If you wanted my attention, all you had to do was call. We could've had a private conversation. I would have liked that. Because I like to remember the good times. In the end, all you have are the good memories. In fact, I even have a memento. …You wore it whenever you were off duty. Remember? On our last night together? I always wanted to give it back. But you wouldn't talk to me after, so… But don't worry. I wiped it clean. Because the truth is, I'm smarter than you, and you don't have jack shit on me. You're too stupid and weak, which is how you got into this mess, and now you're going to drop this case for lack of evidence. I can just feel it in my bones.

For information on this author,
click on the WRITERS tab at www.smithandkraus.com.

# THE PARIS OF THE WEST

*David MacGregor*

Dramatic
Jimmy Floyd, thirty to fifty

*At 3:00 a.m. in Bronco's Lounge, a bar across the street from the Ford River Rouge Plant, autoworker Jimmy Floyd toasts his last day on the job with Meg, the owner/bartender.*

## JIMMY FLOYD

In this country there is nothing more obsolete than a factory rat like me. You're looking at a museum piece. A relic of a bygone age. I'm telling you, the moment I drop dead some guys from the Smithsonian are gonna scoop me off the pavement, stuff me, and put me on display. Rodentus Factorius Americanus. Thrived in the Midwestern United States during the twentieth century. Now extinct. I'll be in a glass case with the woolly mammoth and the fucking dodo bird. Shit, maybe it's all for the best, because people these days have no fucking idea about the factory…what it does to you. I mean, you hit that assembly line on your first day and you're like any other loser. You hate the spics, you hate the niggers, you hate whitey, you hate the faggots, and you hate all the bitches and assholes who have fucked you over for your entire life. And you get into that factory for a few months and all that just drops away and you realize you only have one enemy in this universe, one enemy that keeps coming for you day after day and week after week and that you hate more than you ever thought you could hate anything and it's the clock. That factory clock that hangs over your head and your station and your life, the second hand dragging its way around and around that dial and slowing down every time you look at it and so you train yourself to not look at it, to not stare into the eyes of God because that clock is your God and it's a God that wants to punish you for ever being born. So you're at your station four or five hours into your shift and your muscles are aching and your mind is screaming at the monotony of it all and so you do the only thing you can do and you start repeating your mantra, the chant of every line worker across the world, and it's like a heartbeat inside you and it's fuck them fucking fuckers. Fuck them fucking fuckers. Fuck them fucking fuckers. And the guy next to you says fuck them fucking fuckers and down the line you hear fuck them fucking fuckers and now everyone is saying it or yelling it or pounding it out on their benches. Fuck them fucking fuckers. Fuck them fucking fuckers! Fuck them fucking fuckers!!! And it's not just you and the machine and it's not you against the machine, you are the machine, just another fuck them fucking fuckers cog in this huge fuck them fucking fuckers machine and you pound out your minutes and your days and your life in that machine and every second that you're pounding it, it's pounding you and then one day your life goes by and you're done. The machine spits you out on the sidewalk and you lay there staring up at a sky you've never seen and it hits you, hits you like a poleaxed pig in a fucking slaughterhouse just how fucking done it is and how fucking done you are. So there you go…that's my shop rat wisdom wrapped up in a thank you for your service certificate and a shiny new lapel pin. Now give me another fucking beer.

# POET ON A STRING

*Richard Vetere*

Dramatic
Delmore, late twenties-early thirties

*The poet Delmore Schwartz is speaking to his wife, Gertrude Buckman. Schwartz pleads with Gertrude to stay with him in a scene where she tells him she is leaving him and breaking up their marriage.*

## DELMORE

Look at you. Smirking at me. What, you don't believe I deserve such influential enemies? What little you know. My name strikes fear in the hearts of the mighty. They dread my talent like Egyptians feared the plague of locusts. And you thought you married a nobody? Thee of little faith. (pause) He'll only think of you as his whore. His precious Jewish whore. But to me you are my raven haired-goddess. You inspired and enthralled me. (pause) You're wrong. You are beautiful. And you're face alone would inspire a world of poetry. If only I had told you that before this night. (pause) If I had liked your short stories, would you have stayed? I should have lied and told you that you, Gertrude, my Gerty, you are a great writer. Of course it would have made a difference. You would have loved me more. You would have thought of me as caring and nurturing. Instead, what do I do? I give you the truth. I tell you that you have no talent. How stupid can I be? I should have lied. I should have lied like they all lie. I gain nothing but telling you the truth. All I do is show my ego, is that not what you're thinking? He has to tell me that I have no talent because it makes him look more important? I know that's what you're thinking and it's true. I have the gift and you don't. Wanting it doesn't give it to you. It takes monumental dedication and genius to be me. A genius is born and talent needs blood and sweat to grow. You are ordinary, Gerty. There's no shame in that but that's not what you want to hear. Why didn't I just tell you that you, too, are a genius? Why couldn't I do that? I love you. I love you more than my own being and yet I couldn't lie for your sake. I deserve this pain I feel now in losing you. My integrity has no value when faced with losing you. I should have told you what you wanted to hear.

# PRICELESS

_David Robson_

Dramatic
Arthur, forties-fifties

_Arthur, a shady art expert, speaks to amateur art thieves who believe they've stolen a masterpiece. He's attempting to justify the work he does appraising art for European Mafiosi._

## ARTHUR

I long ago reconciled the fact that people are different; from time to time their needs or wants intersect, but I don't hold their lack of interest in aesthetics against them. Why should I? They're little different from most of the rest of the world. People see the Mona Lisa and ooh and aah over it, as if they know what makes it a masterpiece. They have no clue, but this is what they've been told is worthy—this is what they've been told art is. They have no original ideas on the subject, only what they've have digested from television documentaries and art history classes at their local community colleges. But you can't blame them. Who has time for art? Life is hard and art, for most, is a luxury occasionally jammed between work, sleep, food, sex, and baseball games. Anyway, can you imagine a world full of art experts blathering on about negative space and abstraction and Picasso's evolution from realism to Cubism? How abominable a world that would be, eh?

# PRICELESS

*David Robson*

Dramatic
Zacke, thirties

*Zacke, an amateur art thief hired by his old friend Raymond to steal a priceless painting from Raymond's mistress, tells the story of breaking into the mistress's apartment.*

## ZACKE

I knew where she probably had the painting. You told me to look in the red armoire. And so I took my time—looked at her books on the shelf. I always wanted to read more, you know. But, I don't know, I'd always start one and then lose interest. She really likes books. After a while, I wandered into her bedroom. I saw the red armoire. It was where you said it would be, but I didn't rush. I smelled some of the perfume bottle she had on her vanity—smelled pretty good. I even tried one. I had no worries. She could have been home any minute, but for some reason I just didn't hurry. She had that picture of the two of you on her nightstand. I was going to take it, like you said, but it was weird. It just looked so perfect sitting there. She looked so happy; you looked so happy. I couldn't bring myself to take it. I mean, here I was standing in her bedroom, standing where you probably stood a million times. I didn't look at the bed, don't worry. It just didn't feel right. I mean, here I was on a mission to kill this woman and steal her secret family heirloom, so to look at her bed—where the two of you were together. Who was I to judge her? I was the same as she was—right—as you were? So, I don't know. I opened the armoire; it wasn't locked, and I took out the suitcase. I kept wondering why she'd keep a thing like that in there, but she did anyway. And here it is. She probably doesn't even know it's gone yet. But none of it matters now anyway. We sold the fucking thing!

# RABBI SAM

## Charlie Varon

Comic
Bob Lew, sixties

*Bob Lew is the chairman of the synagogue's board of directors. He has just arrived, late, to the first board meeting with the new rabbi, and discovered a big, messy argument. Bob wants everyone to be happy, will do anything to defuse conflict, and has a big, East Coast Jewish voice and sense of humor.*

### BOB

You know what - we're gonna be nice for a little while. We're gonna be civil. My fault. My fault. I was late. I almost forgot the refreshments, then I was late. Uhright, has everybody got coffee? Help yaself if ya need more coffee. There's also juice. And let me give you a guided tour of the food. Jews meet, we need food, we need fuel. We have a rabbi, friends, who's a New Yorker, I want to apologize in advance for the bagels – these are not New York bagels. These are Noah's bagels, they call 'em New York bagels but they're *not*! They put something in the Noah's bagels. They put dough conditioners. *(Laughing.)* Who knew from dough conditioners – when the ancestors in Poland were making bagels, they didn't have dough conditioners! But the pastries, Rabbi, taste the pastries, you won't be disappointed. The pastries will make you glad you moved to California because the fruit is better: This is an apricot danish. This is a cherry danish. This is a blueberry danish. This is what they call a breakfast roll it's pretty good, and there a couple of croissants. I mean, realistically, folks, should we not have *champagne*?! New rabbi, first board meeting! I raise my cup to you, Rabbi Sam, I apologize it's just coffee. Glad you came today, Rabbi? Glad you took the job? Ya still want it, Rabbi? *(He laughs.)* I don't wanna lose you before ya practically started. You walked into the lion's den, Rabbi, maybe you oughta change your name to Daniel, Daniel in the lion's den, huh? But in point of fact we don't throw anybody to the lions; we're not Romans, and you're obviously not a Christian ha ha – So Rabbi, welcome; I recommend the bear claws; I do *not* recommend the cheese danish! They're terrible. *(He laughs uncontrollably.)* I'm lying, rabbi! Everybody knows I'm lying! Except you. Cheese danish!.

*(Makes a noise and gestures with hands.)* Uhhh-hhh. I love cheese danish! My absolute, absolute weakness! *(Suddenly quiet.)* On this board of directors, I'm gonna be very serious for just a moment, on this board of directors, we have no secrets. Except one. *(Earnestly.)* Nobody tells my wife how many cheese danish I eat. Or my cardiologist. What I eat – stays in this room – are we agreed? Do I have your agreement, Rabbi? I'd like a verbal assent, not just a nod. Thank you.

# RABBI SAM

## Charlie Varon

Seriocomic
Rabbi Sam, early to mid-forties

*Rabbi Sam Isaac is giving his first sermon to his new congregation. Rabbi Sam's impulse is to create a Judaism that's like jazz – an improvisation on tradition. His sermons should have the feeling of jazz – unscripted, discovered in the moment, developing and improvising on themes, letting the "music" flow through him. He is a soloist who enjoys the range of his "instrument" – high and low notes, fast and slow, loud and pianissimo. But Sam is always aware of his audience. He uses the entire stage when he gives his sermons. Those sermons should feel passionate, alive and dangerous. If he has a hero in the world of jazz, it might be Thelonious Monk.*

## RABBI SAM

Jews 3000 years from now: what do they want from us? We have been trained to think about religion in the past tense. We can imagine Moses 3000 years ago, but Jews 3000 years *from* now – go ahead, imagine it. You can't. I can't. Gesher. Gesher. We're the bridge. Last Sunday I went and checked out the *(mischievous)* competition. I went to three different churches in this community. Do you know which service was the most grab-your-kishkes? A Baptist fundamentalist church – this was a white church, by the way... I'll give you the upshot of that service: You and I are going to roast in hell. The fundamentalists have put the car in reverse; they're going 80 miles an hour back to the year 1900. Or further. But they are on *fire*! Synagogues in America – also stuck in the past. Gutless, going through the motions – you know what I'm talking about – Museum Judaism. And you know what the worst is? When they throw in just a pinch of that shtetl kitsch. *(Mocking.)* Oh, it's almost Shabbos and the hard-working papa has *almost* enough money to buy a chicken for the Shabbos meal, but it's getting dark, the sun is going down... I promise: I will never indulge in nostalgia. Tevye is not going to save us.

# RABBI SAM

*Charlie Varon*

Seriocomic
Rabbi Sam, early to mid-forties

*Rabbi Sam Isaac is giving his first sermon to his new congregation. Rabbi Sam's impulse is to create a Judaism that's like jazz – an improvisation on tradition. His sermons should have the feeling of jazz – unscripted, discovered in the moment, developing and improvising on themes, letting the "music" flow through him. He is a soloist who enjoys the range of his "instrument" – high and low notes, fast and slow, loud and pianissimo. But Sam is always aware of his audience. He uses the entire stage when he gives his sermons. Those sermons should feel passionate, alive and dangerous. If he has a hero in the world of jazz, it might be Thelonious Monk.*

## RABBI SAM

Each of our lives – is a river. Flowing toward the ocean. And yeah, the ocean is death. All we have, chaverim, all we have is *Ehiyeh asher ehiyeh*, becoming that which we cannot yet imagine. And you know how light dances on a river at sunset? God watching us. One night Thomas Jefferson took a scissors to his Bible. Do you all know this? Jefferson went through and he literally cut out of the Bible everything that made no sense to him. He cut out the virgin birth of Jesus. We must have the courage of Jefferson, but instead of a scissors ... See, Jefferson did not have a personal computer, did not have... what's it called when you change the size of the type? Fonts! Scalable fonts! We need a Torah with scalable fonts. *(Hands indicate big)* – *Ehiyeh asher ehiyeh* in – 50,000-point type. And then in teensy weensy little 2-point type: *"Zot ha b'heyma asher tocheylu"* – "These are the animals you may eat." We don't cut those words out of Torah. Why? Our river did not start with us. We need to know the longer river that we are part of. But we also need to let the river flow forward. *Ehiyeh asher ehiyeh*. Judaism: First civilization to believe that human beings shape history! Yeah. Take a minute with that. In 1776 the Continental Congress assembled in Philadelphia to design, to conceive, to imagine, to invent! – Their question: What is a nation? The essential creative act of our country was a Jewish act! Frederick Douglass, Harriet Tubman, Abraham Lincoln: freeing the slaves: a Jewish act! Elizabeth

Cady Stanton, Susan B. Anthony: giving women the vote: Jewish! America's greatness: acts of stepping out of the confines of what had seemed immutable. Which makes America what? *(Pause.)* A Jewish nation. They do not yet teach this in the public schools. One day they will. And I, for one, think Judaism can hold its own in the marketplace of ideas. Beloved, do you see the lineage we stand in? As Jews. As Americans. As *American Jews!* The Great Seal of the United States: The bald eagle. You know, that's not what Ben Franklin wanted. You know what Franklin wanted on the Great Seal? *Moses!* Moses with his arm outstretched and the Egyptian army drowning in the sea! Not the Crucifixion, not the Resurrection, not Jesus: Moses. America is a Jewish nation: somebody needs to tell Pat Robertson. Is there something we can sue him for? Copyright infringement? America – I'm gonna get in trouble for this – America *(quietly)* is the *most* Jewish nation. *Ehiyeh asher ehiyeh.* Water. Water, beloved, water. Can we be like water?

# THE RIGHT KIND OF PEOPLE

_Michael Weems_

Dramatic
Ronnie, thirty-five - forty

_Ronnie reflects on the holidays with his roommate Tim and Tim's new girlfriend Eva._

## RONNIE

So, let's set the scene: Year: 2006. Junior Year of college. I'm kind of in a really weird place. Dad laid off from a company where he worked for over thirty years and my sister had just gotten married for the third time by age twenty five; my a-hole Granddad who'd considered me a failure ever since birth was fading; and I'd broken up with this girl Kelsey. Things just hit a wall. I started thinking long term and just couldn't see how we could make things work beyond casual hook ups and she didn't want to break up at all – wanted to get hitched actually. We made a plan to sit and talk about this over Thanksgiving.So it's a situation of traveling down the highway towards something you really don't want. It was probably about 9:30 pm and I decided to pull off on a random feeder to get some gas and a Coca Cola. Across the street, I saw my beacon. A strip club. It wasn't like sex wasn't on the plate with Kelsey, but it was the perfect distraction. The parking lot was pretty bare, but I took my chances. I opened the door ...The club...oh hot damn. It's sad inside. There's a bar up the left side with maybe one patron and a lonely, ugly bartender. In the middle, a stage. On the right, 'V.I.P' room – separated from the 'action' by a red curtain. I order a beer from the ugly bartender and watch the 'show' start. She's thirty. At least. She's not terrible but not great. Her implants haven't seen a surgeon's blade in way too long. Her skin looks like West Palm Beach at Sunday Brunch. But, it's an escape. She's got the 1,000 yard stare down pat. Dancer #2 enters and the situation is still bad. She's of some arguable Latin descent, though not without semi mustache, stretch marks, multiple visible tattoos, and just when I'm even barely caring enough to check for an Adam's Apple – I start to leave...only to be interrupted by dancer #1. Taffy. She smiles and asks where I'm going. Clearly someone who has time to kill on a pre-Thanksgiving night has a few more minutes. And did I go to college? She knows the game and isn't playing dumb. She talks about younger lovers she's had. Taffy asks, that if I'm not feeling too thrifty if I might join her in the VIP. Done deal. The back room: Again, technique and grace aren't the faults here. She's deliberate and slow, but purposeful. She keeps sayin' over and over "You're such a good boy. I like the good boys. I get the bad boys all the time and they paw me like a dollar steak tossed out by the butcher." After dance number two she smiles and thanks me for being one of the good ones. A few bills exchange and she's gone. I head straight for my car. The only remedy is to roll the windows down, blast music, and pretend like this was all okay. I popped into my parents' home and said hi and bye, assuring them I'd help cook in the morning. Met Kelsey, assured her we were fine. And proceed to bump uglies in the the back of her Mercedes. The aftermath: Dated Kelsey through the holidays and eventually broke up. Now dating Taffy and going strong. tHappy Thanksgiving to me.

# THE RIGHT KIND OF PEOPLE

*Michael Weems*

Dramatic
Tim, twenty-five to thirty-five

*Tim is overheard bragging about injuring an opposing player in a hockey game by his girlfriend Eva. When she confronts him, he responds about who he really is.*

## TIM

We're just the schlubs. Blue collar. White trash even. We can't afford the good beer. We're probably going to end up living in this place together until one of us dies...that's just the way it is. I'm not perfect. I know this. I like hockey. I like the bruises and the adrenaline and the fights. To you, that means I'm going to come home and beat up everything with a pulse and two legs. t's just not true. Last year, Ronnie and I went to this game. The team drafted this young hayseed, probably about six and a half feet tall, couple hundred pounds, just a good ol' corn fed boy who probably had a single digit IQ. So this little runt on the other team is all over him. All. Friggin. Game. He's chippin' on him. Slashing him when the ref's not looking. Hitting him square in the few places he doesn't have pads. By the second period, hayseed's looking pissed. Like David and Goliath or something. Finally, the runt rushes at him and drops his gloves. The guy extends his tree trunk of an arm and stops the kid. He looks around and the refs are already there just waiting...they know it's gotta happen and they just shrug. He wings his meaty fist straight down on top of this kid's head. He's out cold. No blood, no broken bones, just a message sent: the meek might inherit, but they ain't getting by without learning a lesson. This is how we have to live. We're the big dumb lug, constantly pestered by the runt bosses, landlords, relatives until we can't take any more. When some other little runt infested our game, our one true release from this shit world, I defended it. At the end of the day, he'll go back to his trophy wife and car dealerships and his huge bank account, but we protected our integrity. We saw through the bullshit and handled it like men when the voice of reason wouldn't work. If you really think all that other stuff, you just don't know me.

# THE RIGHT KIND OF PEOPLE
_Michael Weems_

> Dramatic
> Ronnie, thirty-five to forty

_After witnessing a fight between his roommate Tim and Eva (Tim's now ex-girlfriend), Ronnie sits Eva down and challenges her perception of what a 'nice guy' really is._

## RONNIE

Let me set the stage for you. So, after I broke up with the girl, and started hounding Taffy, life changed a bit. I'd never pursued a girl like this. Maybe it was just wanting to date a stripper – a notch on the belt. So, I'm trying my best - wooing her and all. I had to pay off a few of her friends to find out that she didn't have a boyfriend. We ended up boozing at a party and while nothing really happened, we hit it off and agreed to see a movie the next week. Blah blah blah, hit it off, first date, 'officially dating,' fast forward a few months ahead. Everything was going pretty smoothly. What happens next is one of those moments where looking back, I should probably feel some shame. And yet, I don't. At this same time was this guy in the club – a regular who always pined for Taffy – let's call him Mitch. Fat, asexual, odd, friendly – surrounded by his huge posse of fat/asexual/friendly leeches. He always had that unrequited/one sided adoration for her and all of his friends knew it. Bottom line - she was out of his league and even if I weren't in the picture, she wasn't attracted to him. One of the outliers of this group was one of Taffy's friends, Scott. Scott let me know that Mitch was planning on personally going back to her dressing room that night and basically letting all his feelings out, get on one knee, and pray for the best. I took this to heart. I decided we should do some shots that night. I bought round after round for anyone who'd look me in the eye...especially Taffy. She's giggly by the time we get back to her dressing room and I remind her that it's my birthday....it wasn't. The shots worked. Later I was informed that Mitch got about three feet from the door and was found crying amongst his asexual/fat/friends. Bottom line: I orchestrated drunk sex with the girl he thought he loved and made sure he heard her during. I am not a nice person. Tim _is_ a nice person. Most men are _not_ nice people. We see something bright and shiny in our peripheral, whether it be car or bike or TV, and life becomes keeping up with the Jones' by any means necessary. He who ends up with the most toys...wins.

# RULES OF COMEDY
## *Patricia Cotter*

Comic
Guy, mid to late-twenties

*Guy doesn't make much money as a stand-up comic, so he does one-on-one coaching sessions. He has run up against a brick wall with Caroline, who just isn't funny.*

## GUY

I probably should have cancelled, but you know, I needed the a hundred and fifty bucks. Look, I understand if this isn't your thing. As a matter of fact, I'm gonna give you a hundred back right now and we can call it a night. Basically I just gave you a one-on-one tutorial, a hundred seems fair to me. I am just going to be brutally honest, Caroline. You're not funny. At all. You actually would be a nightmare to even have in the audience. You can't question, or worry about why a rabbi would walk into a bar, or why a cowboy would have a parrot on his shoulder, you just have to go with it. I don't know about perfect, but if I give you a good example, you'll leave? Just so you know, this isn't one of my jokes. I do more, like, stories from my life. Well, you know, you heard... whatever. But this is a classic, well-built joke, this is basically the Toyota Camry of jokes. A couple of New Jersey hunters are out in the woods when one of them just all of a sudden collapses and falls to the ground. His friend checks him out - and the guy doesn't seem to be breathing, his eyes are rolled back in his head - it looks pretty bad. So the hunter, completely freaked out, whips out his cell and calls 911. He gets the operator and says: "Help me. I think my friend is dead! What do I do?" The operator says: "Just take it easy, sir. I can help. The first thing we need to do is to make sure your friend is dead." So the guy pulls out his rifle and shoots his friend. Then he comes back on the line, and says to the operator: "OK, he's definitely dead. Now what?"

Lawrence Harbison

# THE SADTIC EP

*Graham Techler*

Seriocomic
Abish, mid-twenties

*Abish, a go-getter who has recently moved back into his parents' house, is working on an acoustic punk EP with his passionate—if a little unstable—friend, Eli. When they call an old high school acquaintance in to help them find musical inspiration, her lack of familiarity with the genre prompts Abish to launch into a rapid history of punk music and its various offshoots.*

## ABISH

You see, Mercer, punk started in the 1970s, coming out of garage rock and things like that. It was a genuine phenomenon in the U.K. especially, as well as in the U.S. This is where we get the anti-authoritarian ideology of punk from bands like the Sex Pistols and the Clash! This is also where we get punk clothing and subculture, and where punk becomes—largely—shining, porcelain, lily-white. But when the 80s came and anything became fair game right before the MTV era, punk music split in two, heading down very different paths. One half of punk gave rise to the first wave hardcore movement in America, mostly California, as well as the subgenre "Oi!" in Britain. This would further develop into thrash, and then combine with 70s stadium rock to create modern heavy metal and speed metal. But that does not concern us right now at all. On the other side of the aisle, people who loved punk went on to follow a post-punk tangent and create the far more commercially popular alternative rock movement. For instance, Nirvana, grunge, all that stuff. Weezer creates emo music and then disappears to let it ruin itself. Now *this* is where it gets really complicated, as both these subgenres divide fairly uncleanly into either melodic punk or a-melodic punk, and a gazillion other subgenres appear. On the amelodic side of things, garage punk and glam punk spiral back to the 60s influence and take a lot of clues from psychedelia. A subsection of that disappears *wayyyy* up its own ass to become avant-garde art punk. Then a-melodic punk splits *again* to become political and apolitical. Minor Threat famously declares themselves a straight-edged punk group, creating the all too common occurrence of an awesome band inadvertently creating a monster, in this case: Christian punk. Similarly, thrash goes a little too far and becomes Nazi punk. Both of these things suck equally. Thrash then goes too far in another direction and becomes gutter-punk, which in some circles is just known as "stylish homelessness." However! You also have afro-punk, like Death from Detroit, the progressive Islamic "taqwacore," queercore, peace punk, and anarcho punk, which advocates anarchy. These are far more palatable, but none of them more fantastic than "Riot Grrrl!" That's G-R-R-R-L, thank you very much. This was hardcore feminist punk genre that peaked in the 90s but we still got Sleater-Kinney and Bikini Kill out of it! And it just goes to show that women can be punk rock, too!

# THE SADTIC EP
## Graham Techler

Seriocomic
Eli, mid-twenties

*Eli, an emotionally unstable slacker, has moved back to his hometown along with his friend Abish with the hopes of recording the Great American Acoustic Punk EP, a DIY masterpiece that will put them both on the map. However, once the EP is actually finished, both Abish and the duo's muse-turned-bassist Mercer can't defend the album's aggressive self-indulgence. A self-indulgence Eli feels deserves a passionate defense.*

### ELI

You know. Statistically the first thing you ever did was cry for no reason. Can you give me one time you've been happy since the last time you got to whine completely unselfconsciously, when you were, what, nine? Ten? That's what we do! That's what we're supposed to do! Yes nobody wants to hear about it and yes it's a dumb idea to put that out into the world! But goddamn it! I want to be dumb! I'm dumb! And you are too, you phonies! Well I'm not gonna stand for it anymore. I HAVE SEX! WITH PEOPLE I DON'T LIKE! SO I'LL FEEL BETTER ABOUT MYSELF! I THINK OTHER PEOPLE ARE OUT TO GET ME! I'M JEALOUS OF THE SUCCESSFUL BECAUSE I CONSIDER THEM A MASSIVE THREAT TO MY WAY OF LIFE, AND I DON'T WANT PEOPLE TO LEAVE ME ALONE IN FAVOR OF THEM. I'M JEALOUS OF PEOPLE IN THEIR THIRTIES WITH.... NICE WATCHES. I NEVER WANT ANYONE I KNOW TO ASSOCIATE WITH PEOPLE OF MONEY OR CLOUT BECAUSE IF THEIR PERSONALITY IS GOOD THEN THEY'RE JUST OVERALL BETTER THAN ME BECAUSE FOR A LONG TIME ALL I'VE HAD GOING FOR ME IS MY PERSONAL-ITY AND I'M SLOWLY REALIZING THAT MY PERSONALITY LEAVES A LOT TO BE DESIRED. And if you don't want to hear about it then too fucking bad. You see, boys forget what their country means by just reading The Land of the Free is history books. Then they get to be men; they forget even more. Liberty's too precious a thing to be buried in books, Miss Mercer. Men should hold it up in front of them every single day of their lives and say "I'm free to think and speak." My ancestors couldn't, I can, and my children will. Boys ought to grow up remembering that. I guess this is just another lost cause, Abish. All you people don't know about lost causes. Mr. Abish does. He said once they were the only causes worth fighting for and he fought for them once. For the only reason any man ever fights for them. Because of just one plain simple rule. Love thy neighbor. And in this world today of great hatred a man who knows that rule has a great trust. You know that rule, Mr. Abish, and I loved you for it just as my father did. And you know that you fight harder for the lost causes than for any others. Yes you'd even die for them. Like a man we both knew, Mr. Abish. You think I'm licked. You all think I'm licked. Well I'm not licked. And I'm gonna stay right here and fight for this lost cause. Even if this room gets filled with lies like these. And the Mercers and all their armies come marching into this place. Somebody will listen to me! So you say it's self- indulgent! Do you remember how good self-indulgence feels!? It's the most pleasing thing that's ever existed on Earth!

# SLOW NIGHT IN ELK CITY

## *Sam Bobrick*

Dramatic
J.G., late fifties

*J.G., a barber, speaks to Carl and Francis Lemay, the owners of a small town bar he frequents. It is the mid-seventies and the town of Elk City has fallen on hard times J.G. is complaining about how everything in the country is changing, even the barbershop business.*

### J.G.

*(building to a tirade)*

You know what the problem is? Loyalty! Today, people got no loyalty to anything. I only have half the customers I once had and you know why? 'Cause going to a plain old barber like me isn't good enough for them anymore. Today they need to go to a hair stylist. Cost three times as much, takes four times as long cause you have to use hair sprays and hair nets and hair dryers and all kinds of sissy colognes and you gotta clip their nose hairs and cut their eye brows and it's pampering and ass kissing and more pampering and more ass kissing and God forbid you nick an ear you'll never hear the end of it. Well, I can't bring myself to do that kind of barbering because it ain't right and it ain't barbering, not for a real man's haircut, the kind I've been giving for the last thirty years and will continue to give until the day they carry me away so I say screw them. I've got my pride.

# SLOW NIGHT IN ELK CITY
## Sam Bobrick

Dramatic
Teddy, mid-forties

*Teddy works in the Personnel Dept of a corporation located in Elk City, a small town that has fallen on hard times. It is the mid-seventies and Teddy's explaining to his friends at the bar he frequents about how corporations are beginning to cut down on the use of workers.*

### TEDDY

They don't want anyone over thirty. Isn't my idea. Company policy. Besides, it isn't what you know that they're interested in. They just need a couple of strong backs for the warehouse. Anything that takes any intelligence they got operating by computer. It's just a matter of time before they're gonna have computers running those computers. It's happening at all the big companies. The average working guy in this country is headed for the shit heap. The good jobs are going, the pensions are going and the poor bastards they let go know they're never gonna find jobs like they lost. I blame it on the government. They're doing nothing to stop progress. Why should they give a damn? They're getting theirs and that's all they care about. Yeah, things are changing and I don't think for the better. They're even starting to send some of the work overseas cause it can get done cheaper. It's all about making as much money as they can now. No, the writing's on the wall. Things are changing and I'm not sure it's for the best.

Lawrence Harbison

# STET

## *Kim Davies*

Dramatic
Connor, twenty-one

*Connor is a student activist and the vice president of a fraternity, venting his frustration with what he views as the out-of-touch sexism of the reporter interviewing him.*

## CONNOR

You're really sexist. Look, I'm the one going into frat houses, talking to sports teams, talking to dudes about this stuff, and I know that I'm not making a huge difference or anything, but the thing is—guys are really ready to hear this. They want to talk about consent. We're not a bunch of fucking rapists waiting to happen. We want everybody to have a good time. I think you're being sexist against women, actually. Because, like, we go to college with women. We know what women are like. Because they're like us, you know? Do you have any fucking idea how stressful college is right now? And forget high school. I was salutatorian of my class, I played three sports, I had to get a 33 on the ACT—I nearly had a fucking nervous breakdown just trying to get here. And like, I know I joke around and stuff, but college is harder. Because it doesn't end here, right? There's law school or business school or med school, or there's getting the first job or the right internship or whatever—I know I'm going to be clawing my way up that ladder for the rest of my life. So if I have four years where I can do that and also hang out with my friends and get wasted, I'm going to do that. And all the girls I know feel the same way. Look, I'm not going to pretend I haven't seen some fucked-up shit. I know I live in a frat house. Not a nun house. Like yeah, I think there are shitty guys. I know there are shitty guys out there. what I want is to make their behavior less normal, so like you see that shit and you're not like, whatever, guys suck, but you're like *that guy sucks* and he needs to *stop*. This is on guys, you know? It's on us to change. I just don't see women as victims waiting to happen.

For information on this author,
click on the WRITERS tab at www.smithandkraus.com.

# STRAIGHT

## Scott Elmegreen and Drew Fornarola

Dramatic
Ben, twenty-six

*Ben is dating Emily but he's very attracted to a younger guy named Chris.*
*Ben is conflicted about his sexuality. Here, he tells Chris why.*

### BEN

How many people, in the world, besides the guys, obviously, know you've done stuff like And how many family members? And why is that? Answer my question! It's because if people knew, you'd stop being Chris who goes to Boston College, who studies history, who likes the kinds of music you like and hates the kinds of movies you hate, and you'd just be gay Chris, the gay friend, and there'd be no going back, even if later you decided you were tired of being just that It's because we're obsessed with drawing neat little lines around things. Dichotomizing. People don't like ambiguity. A guy is straight by default. If he does something with another guy, he goes over to gay, and that's it, everything attached. Of course [your friends'd] be cool with it— they'd be fucking fascinated! That's my point. They'd think you're going on this amazing adventure, like to Japan, or something. They'd wanna know allll about who's gay, who might be, who is but doesn't know it yet—*as if that's even a thing*— and it'd be all fun and games till it hits too close to home. *Yes,* fucking Japan! This exotic adventure where you *find* yourself and come to *terms* with things and bring back rousing details and secrets about the way the other half lives. And everyone's so excited for you! It's not being able to look away. Who's gonna be the next one to turn? The pop singer? The kooky friend? It's a veritable game show! But wait, no, not our son. Not my brother. Suddenly it's "Are you sure?" and "Where did I go wrong?" because that's *real*. It's like the goddamn Pink Scare in America. We don't know what we're supposed to think. "Oh, but it's cool that my friend is. Yeah, yeah, my coworker's that way, that's fine. He's a really nice guy." Everyone wants gay friends but no one wants gay kids.

For information on this author,
click on the WRITERS tab at www.smithandkraus.com.

# THE TALENTED ONES
*Yussef El Guindi*

Dramatic
Omar, late twenties

*Omar is having an all-out fight with his wife, Cindy. He caught her making out with his good friend Rick, and she just found out he's been fired from his job.*

## OMAR

I want you to stop thinking I'm the worst thing that ever happened to you. It pours out of you, all the time, in little ways. I didn't know it was possible to tyrannize another human being with so much selflessness. The way you give of yourself until there's nothing more important happening than what you're doing for the other person. I don't mean that in a snide way but your love seems so dependent on my being a loser that I feel I would be betraying something in our marriage if I actually succeeded. I think you'd be dumbstruck if I succeeded. And most of all you can avoid facing your own shortcomings. Am I really the reason you don't pursue your dancing? How handy I must be for that. Perhaps you need to keep your dancing only a fantasy because in the cold light of day it doesn't amount to much. You could dance, but could you compete? How good are you really? You never have to find out because your handful of a husband keeps you distracted. I'm trying to free you. You do need to settle down and start your life with a stable, straight-arrow kind of guy like Rick. Now there's a man with a plan. There's something very masculine, and salt-of-the-earth about Rick. And he's management now. He could provide you with the kind of stability you need. And with me out of the way … I want you to start over. There's no greater magic than starting over, right? Reinventing, claiming our futures. That's what we both talked about. I know: me and your poor family who've been the recipient of your admirable efforts. How they must look up to you. The dutiful daughter who looks after them. That's your real talent looking after sad, struggling cases. Please stop pretending there's some hidden jewel you're hiding that your family or me are stopping you from showing. I know I'm being a shit, I'm sorry. I love you, but sometimes you disappoint me as well. And what I really want now is for you to settle down and be the success story you've always wanted to be, and not just by measuring yourself against me. I'd like to retire my job as the millstone around your neck.

# THE TALENTED ONES
*Yussef El Guindi*

Dramatic
Omar, late twenties

*Underlying this speech are the roiling emotions triggered when Omar saw his wife and his best friend making out through the kitchen window. When he enters the kitchen carrying groceries, they don't know that he's seen them making out. Near the end of the speech he starts referencing that betrayal indirectly.*

## OMAR

Well ... on my way to the store - up on the corner of Jackson and King - did you see the sky about an hour ago? After the rain? The way that low sun was hitting the clouds? Lighting up the wet streets. You couldn't create a more beautiful scene if you tried. So - writer that I am, I took that as a challenge. I went to that coffee place nearby thinking I had plenty of time to get home before you got here, and I, er - I tried to scribble down what I'd seen. That amazing mix of colors. The light bouncing off of windows. And I sat there - I sat there so long trying to come up with something, that I began to be conscious of me sitting there, pen in hand, trying to come up with something. I even started wondering how I must look to anyone watching because I could feel my face pinched in this really concentrated way. This woman, sitting opposite me, I suddenly became self-conscious about how I must look to her, you know, sitting there with my clothes soaked, my hair wet, looking really intense. Even as I tried to capture that sublime scene, I was thinking: "I wonder how I'm coming across to that woman who's watching me." Which completely fucked up the whole sublime thing. Like what a poser, right? And that sudden awareness fucked everything up. And each time I was close to finding just the right combination of words, the experience of trying to find those words, the intensity of it, became like the experience. It completely overwhelmed the amazing thing I'd seen. Which made me get even more self-conscious about what I was doing until the sublime thing I wanted to capture completely slipped away from me and I screamed at that woman to please stop looking at me. *(Slight beat)* Then I left. I came back to apologize, really embarrassed, because she had nothing to do with anything of course. I had done this to myself. I had once again not been able to get out of my own way, you know. Which I know I have to do. But I don't know how you're supposed to really do that. How do I get out of my own way and into that - space where you can truly channel the material you want to get to? That stuff that can pour out of your head and make you go "Wow, did I really write that?" Like none of it really belongs to you, but somehow you've been blessed enough to stumble on to it and claim it as yours. I know I'm not capable of writing stuff like that on my own, but in this other place, if I can get to it, then it happens. Then I'm gunning it down from the first word to the last. And I just thought, fuck: If this is what I love - how can this love so repeatedly fuck me over? You know. How could it betray me to that extent? *I'm* committed to this relationship. But what does this sweet, dear love of mine do? Metaphorically speaking? It picks up this knife; *(Picks up a knife.)* it picks it up, and then stabs me in the back with it. *(He stabs the table.)* And then picks up this salt shaker and pours salt into the wound. *(He has picked up the salt shaker, and pours it where the knife was plunged.)* And then for good measure, it crushes this chili pepper all around the edges of that wound so that the skin swells up in pain and closes around the wound so I can't even get to the very thing that's hurting me like hell, and that I want to write about. What kind of shitty love is that? I ask you.

# THE TALENTED ONES

*Yussef El Guindi*

Dramatic
Omar, late twenties

*Omar and Cindy have each discovered a secret about the other: Cindy has found out that Omar has been hiding the fact that he's been fired from his job, and Omar has caught Cindy making out with his good friend. This is a "dark night of the soul" moment for both of them, where they have to decide if they want to remain together as a couple. Earlier, Omar had confessed that he can't seem to get aroused by her anymore.*

## OMAR

Okay: this is why I can't get a boner. And this may sound meaner than I intend it to be but: there's something about you as a person recently, sometimes, that's really begun to rub me the wrong way. I stress "sometimes" because most of the time I love you; I do. But like -your ambitions for us? All the stuff you want to get. Shopping for furniture we can't afford and then hinting it's my fault that we can't get more in that passive aggressive way of yours. The second car you want, all the goods we apparently swore allegiance to when we raised our hands. The fact that it always comes down to shit we don't have. Stuff we need; the great stack of catalogues, and shopping malls, and credit cards. The lotions you use at night to feel good because the commercial said you would. And now you have the nerve to still talk about wanting to have a career as a dancer? How very inspiring. You *can* have it all because being bloated with fat, stupid meaningless crap is still the prime directive and you're doing a great job at it. I'm saying all this because you hate to see me sit on my feelings so this is me sharing. Because at the end of the day I still - I still love you, most of the time. I wish you the best because you're always trying so very hard for us. If only what you were trying so hard for amounted to more than a pile of worthless *shit*.

# THE TALENTED ONES

*Yussef El Guindi*

Dramatic
Patrick, late twenties

*Patrick is encouraging his good friend's wife to pursue her dancing. He is also trying to seduce her.*

## PATRICK

I've always really liked you Cindy. Not just because you're my buddy's wife. I know I joke around, and I'm sorry about last Sunday, by the way, when you walked in on us. I know it must have sounded crude, the way we talked. But what I'm saying is, that's not me. I actually have like a keen eye and notice shit. And what I've always admired about you is how much you give of yourself to others. Like my mom. - You're a lot sexier than my mom. But you're the same in the way you sacrifice yourself for other people. I used to get so mad at her for not standing up for herself. Her heart was like this big - top-of-the-line Ferrari engine. But it wasn't taking her anywhere, because she was too busy helping other people. Well you know what, I want to be helpful too. I want to pay-it-forward, for all the good things people did for me. I would've stayed in prison for all the dumb shit I did as a kid if it weren't for others helping me out. I know it's not my place to stick my nose in, and maybe all I'll do is let Omar know we talked about this. He has to get a clue at least. It's a sin to walk away from something you love.

# TOLSTOY IN NEW JERSEY

## Sam Bobrick

Comic
Stuart, late twenties to mid-thirties

*Stuart tells the audience what it's like selling women's shoes.*

## STUART

Do you have any idea what it's like selling women's shoes? The crucifixion was a walk in the park. First of all when a woman walks into a shoe store chances are better than good she's depressed. Her life is a fuckin' mess and she's hoping a pair of new shoes will make it all better. She's not sure about the style she wants, or the color she wants, and she probably doesn't even need shoes. But still she makes me bring out every single pair in the store in her size. And with every pair she tries on she walks. She walks up, she walks back, she walks up, she walks back...she walks upi, she walks back. She looks at the heels, looks at the soles, looks at the heels, looks at the soles, walks up and walks back and because she insisted I bring her a shoe a full size smaller than she wears, she stretches every goddamn pair out of shape. Finally, after walking up and back and up and back, her endorphins kick in and suddenly she's feeling better and would rather go out for lunch than buy shoes So she tells me she'll think about it, uses the store's bathroom and leaves. Then I've got to try and squeeze every damn shoe she's tried on back in their box and now because they've all been stretched to another size, they never friggen fit. So I end up breaking the goddamn box and my father slaps me on the head and starts screaming and calling me names like "Dumb Ass" and "Shit For Brains" until another depressed woman walks in and it starts all over again.

# TOLSTOY IN NEW JERSEY
## Sam Bobrick

Comic
Stuart, late twenties to mid-thirties

*Stuart addresses the audience about the failure of our educational system
to consider the needs of the criminal.*

### STUART

Who would have guessed that being cruel, vicious and ruthless
would prove to be my big ticket? As Chekhov once put it so astutely,
being Russian makes you totally adaptable to good and evil. Maybe
that's why I was able to fall into this anti-social niche so effortlessly.
Which got me thinking. Had I started a few years earlier on this path-
way of crime, who knows how much further ahead I would have been
today? I blame this on our out of touch educational system. You see,
early in life we're given aptitude tests to inform us where our best
interests and abilities lie, whether or not we might or might not do
well in professions of our choice, good solid main stream professions
in medicine, government, food service, the arts which usually leads
to food service... And we are encouraged early to put our efforts in
these directions. But what about those who would prefer to take a more
nefarious route such as a jewel thief or bank robber or stock broker? If
someone is gifted with anti-social abilities, why not inform them early
in life so that they too could enjoy the same head start and begin honing
their trade? And by producing better, smarter criminals imagine how
less crowded our prisons would be. In summation let me leave you
with this poignant thought. We are a great nation. If we must produce
scumbags and scoundrels why settle for less than the best? Thank you.

# TRANSit

*Darren Canady*

Dramatic
Lalo, twenties - thirties, Dominican/Black

*New York City. A subway train. After a wiping out on the finale of his routine, street performer Lalo catches Veronica's eye with his skill and energy. Not realizing that Veronica is trans, Lalo finds himself drawn to her as well. However, their interaction – at first flirtatious – turns tense as they interrogate each other more.*

## LALO

Don't lie, mami. Coupla minutes ago you was up there droppin' gutter one second and glamorous the next. Mama got your heels on and whatnot - yeah - but got them thick-ass calves, too. Got those Michelle Obama arms. You ain't always been a lady. You can be Queen Veronica when I'm around, right? Right? Cuz I don't come on like Tito and Darnell and Octavio and alladem. But I know your game, right? Your white boyfriend ain't always with you huh? Sometimes it's just you on the A on the D on the 2 on the 3 - with them fellas you thought I was. And they won't let you be Queen Veronica will they, huh? Yeah - it's Real Raw New York Veronica, right? You can't be Veronica From North Cack-a-fuck then huh? Lemme tell you what Lalo's about: yeah, see the queen from the boonies is cute, but I'm bout this other you, this raw you, this rough you. You don't let no man just grab a fistful of dat ass do you, huh? You don't let no dude down here just take up extra space that's sposed to be yours, do you? Exactly! That's real, you feel me? That's some dangerous shit. That's the only thing that gets me down on to these trains crawlin up in these nasty-ass tunnels - feel the nasty of the city, the danger of it. Feel *alive*. Shit - you think the money is the only reason I do my show? Hell nah - I might fall on my head and snap my neck. Might hit a bar and bust my head open - have blood runnin' off me ev'rywhere. Fuckin crush my spine or somethin. Just when it feels like I might completely fuck myself up, just at that last second when I don't know if there's been enough *propulsion and thrust* - that's when I know I'm alive! That's what you like about me ain't it? Talkin like Queen Veronica now - you playin' the Queen and actin' like Rough And Raw Veronica don't exist! You know I know better - you know we clocked each other - you said you know boys - you know brown boys like me, huh? Right! And you know my moves. Hell you GOT my moves! See, that's why I'm after you right now. That's why I'm still talkin to you, hollerin at you - cuz none of these other chickenheads are worth all this! Been lookin' for a broad like you for a minute - you'll slice a nigga quick as look at him, won't you?

# THE TROUBLE WITH WHERE WE COME FROM

## Scott Caan

Comic
Charlie, mid to late thirties

*Charlie has recently found out his girlfriend, Shelly, is pregnant and didn't have the best reaction to it. Shelly left town and Charlie took the opportunity to invite an old flame, Joanna, to see his play. He is discussing this with his best friend and actor in his play, Vince.*

## CHARLIE

Joanna. Without question, the greatest sex I've ever had in my life. That is, with someone I didn't much care for. This woman did things. I'm telling you. It wasn't something, it was something else. She did things, very amazing things that make people wonder and second-guess how important actually liking someone you are spending time with really is. She's completely out of her mind. She would show up places, and I'm talking about places I didn't even know I was going to, but somehow she did. Stalker type shit. Bunny in the soup type shit, and I was very aware of what I was dealing with, but still, I spent time with this woman. Like on purpose. I was literally scared of this woman, and her actions, like in the real world. Anything not having to do with sex was a complete train accident with this woman, but while and immediately after having sex with her, I would justify spending more time with her. And I knew what the fuck I was doing. I knew the complete disaster of a human being I would be dealing with while dialing her phone number, but I did it anyway. Why? Because it was worth it. It was really something else. Really got ahold of me too. I mean I hate to use the word special... Unique. Very unique. That's better. The things she could manage while nude... You just can't explain it. And it wasn't just what she did or how she looked. No. It was the way she moved. Talked. The way her neck smelled. How her skin felt. *(He starts to melt away into the fantasy, then immediately snaps himself out of it.)* No emotional attachment whatsoever, just so we're clear. I swear to God sometimes I'm not so sure what's stronger, sex or emotional attachment.

For information on this author,
click on the WRITERS tab at www.smithandkraus.com.

# THE TROUBLE WITH WHERE WE COME FROM
## Scott Caan

Comic
Vince, thirties

*Charlie has just told his friend Vince that he needs him to stay at his home because he isn't sure he can trust himself not to cheat on his girlfriend with his ex, Joanna, who may show up at any moment.*

### VINCE

I've been to Prague. It's a small place on the east side of Europe. Where they got girls. Lots of girls. You see a certain lovely bunch of said girls all seem to congregate to these very specific speak easy type of places, but you don't see em at first. No. You walk in, you get a table, and you get a menu. And it ain't a piece of paper. Touch screen menu, handily placed just below the table. You pull it out, the menu I mean, and you get a list. A list of every dream you've ever had, and you get to pick. But you take your time. Why are you talking you're time? A, because you are told to do so, and B, because you are creating the very fantasy that this girl Joanna represents. It's very specific, it is case sensitive, and most of all it's universal. It's a place for men, men like us, men in general. A place where all of your wildest dreams are to be fulfilled, and it is set up in a way that you cannot lose. You are getting exactly what you want. It is there for a reason. Why? So that when you do find the girl to settle down with, you've already had the experience. The very thing we are presently discussing. Now am I implying you should go there and give it a shot? No. In fact I'm saying the exact opposite. You already had it. It's everything that you ever wanted, sexually, only you didn't have to fly 13 hours to get it. But that ain't who you end up with. You just don't. Life don't work that way. You end up with that girl, the one you feel that way about, you end up doing twenty to life on a murder beef. That's Joanna, that's what this is. It's Prague. I get it. I had my version, it's something else, but it's done now. Time to man up. But let's just say you "accidentally" go through with what you are somewhere deep down thinking about going through with here, she might end up being one of your options. And that's no good. Not to mention, on top of all the obvious shit, it's like a rule, or some kind of goofy standard, woman in which you feel so strongly about physically, are never a good match for guys like us. It has something to do with thinking clearly. Not being able to when you're with one of em, I mean. You got a great girl. Do the right thing.

For information on this author,
click on the WRITERS tab at www.smithandkraus.com.

# THE TROUBLE WITH WHERE WE COME FROM
## Scott Caan

Comic
Vince, thirties

*Vince is trying to talk Charlie out of visiting an ex-girlfriend, Samantha, who had broken into Charlie's house earlier that evening to talk to him.*

### VINCE

One more question. Sex with Samantha? How was it? Scale of one to ten. Just curious, but keep in mind we are men so a one is still reason enough to do it again. Worse comes to worse? I'll tell ya. The door's been left open. You walk in. She's nude on the bed. Maybe there's oil and candles. What do I know? You make the wrong decision because you're a human. Shelly finds out, or maybe you tell her, not because it's the right thing to do, but because it somehow makes you feel better, or you thought so anyway. But the inevitable happens. She tells you to beat it, has the baby, and you become one of those fathers that sees their kid every other Sunday, but that gets old and you lose interest because truth be told you were never really a father to begin with. You go through a dark and very deep depression behind the realization you never really worked through your shit, and as a result, basically recreated your own personal shitty childhood experience for your kid to now enjoy too. You live on my couch for a few years, stop writing altogether because it's just too hard to write when you're drinking as heavily as you would be given the circumstance. You sleep with a plethora of hookers, unprotected because that's more fun, and if the STD's don't kill you, you end up putting a bullet in your head. With my gun. It's in the safe next to the bed, but it's never locked. Charlie takes it all in. Just throwin out some ideas. Have fun though. Whatever you do. That's the important thing.

For information on this author,
click on the WRITERS tab at www.smithandkraus.com.

# 23.5 HOURS

*Carey Crim*

Dramatic
Bruce, forties

*Bruce, a teacher and failed novelist, defends a fellow teacher accused of sexual relations with a student.*

## BRUCE

This could have happened to any one of us. This actually *should* have happened to Rich. The way he ogles the cheerleaders. Hell, Ms. Kotcher ogles the cheerleaders. Almost blatantly since she came out. That's not a crime, right? Cheerleaders are meant to be ogled. It's so fucking unfair. You could have been anything but you chose to dedicate your life to those kids. And they burned you for it. My historical detective novel will most likely never get past some junior publisher's slush pile. But you- I didn't know there were people who actually wanted to do this with their lives until I met you. I thought teaching had to be a fallback for everyone else like it was for me. But you made me want to do better. And the fact that you had to go through this hell because some crazy girl... she sure didn't look like a girl. I know how some of those girls can be, Tom. The way they dress. The way they flirt. It's like they *want* you to... it's scary. And you heard about the slut list, right? At Ray's old school? Number one high school in the state, right? Well, it was a hazing thing. The senior girls singled out, I don't know how many freshman, but they wrote down their names with some pretty graphic descriptions of their sexual prowess and then passed the list around school. And, of course, some of the girls were upset to be on the list. Crying, parents outraged, emergency assemblies. But what really stands out for me, what really shines a light, is that a good portion of the freshman girls were upset that they *didn't* make the list. How fucked up is that?

For information on this author,
click on the WRITERS tab at www.smithandkraus.com.

# VAUDEVILLE

## Laurence Carr

Dramatic
Frankie

*In 1919, Frankie Cobb, a vaudeville comic, becomes unhinged when an African-American song and dance man gets a major job offer (to play the Palace, the pinnacle of vaudeville) leaving Frankie behind to address his second rate career.*

### FRANKIE

Did ya hear it? Did ya hear it? Did ya hear the news? God steps out for five minutes to catch a smoke and all hell breaks loose. Did ya hear the news? Did ya hear? Jackie-boy Jackson got the Palace! Laffler handed Jackson the Palace. Laffler handed Jackson the Palace on a silver tray with smoked oysters. I heard it all. I never seen Laffler do such a tapdance. "Mr. Albee wants you for this, Mr Albee'll give you that, come on up to the office for port and cigars. Sign here!" And Jackie-boy just stood there, all eyes and teeth, lookin' like the front end of a Dusenberg. Can you believe it? Jackson! The Palace! What the hell's got into Laffler, anyhow? What the hell's he doin' stickn' his nose on that side of the tracks. He should be lookin' after his own, that's what he should be doin'. Jackie-boy'll get his weeks. All the weeks he wants on the Negro circuit. The T.O.B.A. *(pronounced Toby)* office'll book him up and down the river all season. He doesn't have to horn in on us. I mean. who's runnin' the show here, anyway? What the hell did we fight that war for? To make the world safe for Vaudeville, right? Right, Billy? But what happens? I don't feel safe. Do any of you feel safe? You wake up one day and the world's all cock-eyed. I mean, what am I supposed to do now, black up again and sing a bunch of coon songs.

> *(Sings/Speaks) My gal is a high-born lady, she's black,*
>> *but not too shady.*
>> *Feathered like a peacock and just as gay,*
>> *She ain't colored, she was born that way.*

Jackson. The Palace. Without even tryin''. All I got was the cold shoulder. Laffler was a piece of ice treatin' me like I was the Titanic.

What's wrong with me? I been around, I been here. When did Jackson get ahead of me in line. I've played Vaudeville all over this country. I've played in big houses, middle houses, little houses. If there was a house and some rube put down his two bits, I went out there. Springfield, Scranton, Albany, Patterson, New Haven, Rochester, Buffalo—Buffalo, for Chrissake! I played The Atheneum, and The Grand and The Globe, and the Hip and The Orpheum. I played Zip's Casino in Brooklyn and *they* loved me! Now some leech on Albee's wallet tries to hold out on me. Jackson at the Palace. You know what? I wish he'd walk through that door right now. You know why? I tell you why. So I could look him right in the face and tell him what I think. Right in his black face. Let him in here. I'll give you a little jazzbo! Come on, Jackson. If we were onstage now, you'd be out here. After that buildup. Come on, that's your cue. *(Pause. Nothing happens.)* You see, that's why life stinks. You work up for the big moment, and when it comes—you get nothin'. No payoff. No punch. Just a big, fat nothin'. I'm goin' out for a smoke . . .

For information on this author,
click on the WRITERS tab at www.smithandkraus.com.

# VINO VERITAS
## David MacGregor

Dramatic
Phil, thirties-forties

*Nice guy Phil, the best dad in the neighborhood, reveals his darker side.*

### PHIL

Well, it's not like this makes the nature specials, but you know what a lot of animals are really big on? Killing each other's kids. I'm not talking about different species either. I'm talking about the males going around and killing the babies of other males. It's all about a competition for resources. Monkeys do it, so do fish, whales, insects, cats, dogs, rodents, you name it. If one chimpanzee can bump off another chimp's kid, he'll do it in a heartbeat. I mean, there's only so many antelope out there for the lions, right? Well, for us, there's only so many college scholarships and decent jobs. And these days, let's face it, there are plenty of men who have kids and hit the road. They're not around to protect their offspring, so I say they're taking a big chance. What, you think I'm exaggerating? That I would never seriously contemplate harming a child? Well, let me tell you something. You know that little asshole at the end of the block? Kenny McVee? He's got no Dad, his Mom's at work all the time, so he's basically raising himself. And last year, when Brandon was getting off the school bus at the corner, Kenny took to throwing rocks at him. And Brandon tells me about this, so I go down the next day to see what's happening and sure enough, I see Kenny whipping a rock the size of my fist at Brandon. It hits Brandon on the arm and really staggers the little guy. So I run down there yelling at Kenny and he runs up his driveway onto his porch, opens the storm door, then hides behind the glass giving me the finger. I've got a thirteen-year-old kid who just clocked my son with a rock giving me the finger. And I know what you're thinking. You're thinking I should have called his mother. But I didn't call his mother. I picked up the rock. And Kenny sees this, and he thinks that's hilarious. He thinks he's safe behind the storm door. So now, now he's laughing his ass off and flipping me two fingers. So I wound up and threw that rock as hard as I could. Right through the door, glass shattering all over the porch, all over Kenny, glass everywhere. Then I walked up the driveway and Kenny's just crouched on his porch, shaking like a leaf. And I bent down, and I told him that if he ever bothered my son again, I would break his little fucking neck.

For information on this author,
click on the WRITERS tab at www.smithandkraus.com.

# WAFFLES (or, Scenes from Country Life)
## Graham Techler

Comic
Peter, twenty-seven

*Peter Munn has returned home to Boston on Christmas after a particularly hard go of it in New York. Exhausted, bitter, and irritated, Peter explains his final day in the city to his older brother August.*

### PETER

Okay. My final day in New York was this: I did a reading of Simon's new play at a bar in Bushwick. They paid us with one free drink. I initially picked water because I'm trying to drink less but then changed my mind and tried to order a beer, which they wouldn't give me because I had already used my voucher, even though water is free. They also told Simon that he wouldn't be allowed to do another reading if I was in it because I was 'acting too loud.' Which I would never do unnecessarily. The character demanded it. I then ran into Tim. Who tells me that he's booked a commercial. A national campaign for Wendy's which he had literally found out about earlier that day. Apparently he's going to be playing some loose version of himself which he thinks means he will get to do some improv on set, which is not how that works but he says he needs to "exercise those muscles." He was in the bar because he was there that night that he went in for an audition at the Signature a month after we graduated and confused a black guy for another black guy and thought he'd never work in New York again. That was like five years ago almost to the month so full circle, right? I was at the bar to be paid in water. And I've never had an audition at the Signature. I told him I've always been a Burger King loyalist. Well I thought of it on the J train later, where I fell asleep and woke up about forty minutes from my apartment. Or, Casey's apartment. Which I don't have a key for so I had to let myself in through the window. Casey comes back and accuses me of eating her Nature Valley bars, which I have been but I lied and said I didn't know what she was talking about. So she goes to the trash to pull out a wrapper and flips out because there's trash piled above the rim of the trash can and the one thing she asked me to do was not let trash pile above the rim of the trash can. So I messed up. But I tried to just say I had a really long day, to which she

Lawrence Harbison

says: "Was it long in that you had to listen to a man dying from lung cancer tell you that his daughter wasn't going to be able to visit him from Minneapolis as you put a tube inside his penis? Because that's what I did today." Then she started throwing bonus trash at me. And after a minute or so of having trash thrown at me I decided to leave New York and never come back.

# WARSONG
_Gregory Strasser_

_Steven's wife was murdered, and Ming Jackson has been convicted of the crime. Harry, Ming's son, doesn't believe she did it; nor does Tara, Steven's estranged daughter. They think Steven might have killed her. Here, he tells them that it wasn't him._

## STEVEN

I didn't kill your mother. I almost killed her. I got drunk one night, slept with a hooker, came home and I knocked you senseless. 'Swhy you got that scar on your head. And your mom got in front of me and told me to fuck off, so I beat her. I mean, I beat the shit out of her. I took a fucking pan and smashed her...her face in. And the cops came and I got booked... And when they told me what I did to you two... The restraining order was something I suggested. Your mother kept trying to make it work. She wanted me to come back. She wanted me to start counseling. But I couldn't. I couldn't go back, especially after what I did. So I told her get the restraining order. We needed time. Permanently. You're right, I walked out. But I needed to. If I stayed I'd never gotten clean. Neither would've your mother. And the voicemail was a woman. My sister. It was because we broke our restraining order and I relapsed with Marcy. I would've gone back to jail if anybody had found out. That's why we kept it a secret. You know you're right about one thing, Tara. I'm a piece of shit. I will have always scarred you two, and I'm sorry about that. And I will do anything to right that wrong, and I promise you until my dying day I will never touch liquor again and that I will prevent any more families falling apart like how I made mine. I was a piece of shit, but I did not kill your mother. I loved her. I still love her.

# WASTE LAND

*Don Nigro*

Seriocomic
Pound, mid thirties

*Ezra Pound, poet and enthusiastic and tireless promoter of the works of T. S. Eliot, James Joyce and other great 20th century writers before anyone else had heard of them, is meeting with his friend Eliot and venting his considerable exasperation at the stodgy and conventional literary establishment that seems to block his efforts at every turn. Pound is an enigma. An eccentric and obstreperous American, he has uncanny judgement about great literature, can spot it before anyone else, and his efforts to get Eliot, Joyce and others published are often to the detriment of his own career. Here he has had it with London, and has just about decided it's time to get out of town. Later in his life his eccentricity will turn to something much darker, and cause him to end up in a madhouse, accused of treason and worse. But here he is still his funny and very likable younger self, as he confronts the real issue, which is that the bravest and most interesting artists of any time are often ignored, ridiculed, and thought of by more conventional people as insane.*

## POUND

I've been sending Joyce's *Portrait of the Artist* to one publisher after another, and not one of those blockheads will touch it with a barge pole. Got this report back from the resident cretin at Duckworth, giving helpful suggestions about how it can be trimmed and simplified so as to appeal to the moronic reading public he deludes himself that he's superior to. This is why the good's the enemy of the great. The literary establishment is dominated by high functioning mediocrities. They're fairly intelligent, fairly literate, relatively benign, but show them something a hundred times as good as anything they're publishing and they take an hour patronizing you about how it doesn't quite come up to their standards. Can't we send these god damned lopsided gonads to the Serbian front? I have yet to meet an editor I wouldn't cheerfully fry in oil. This has always been my problem. I have no tolerance for stupidity. In college they told me if I wore red socks they'd throw me in the frog pond. So I wore red socks, and they threw me in the frog pond. The next day I wore red socks again. And they all said, Ezra Pound is crazy. He wants us to throw him in the frog pond. Why the hell would I want them to throw me in the frog pond? It was damned cold in that frog pond. But I had a whole drawer full of red socks, and it seemed like a shame to let them go to waste. So I was blackballed from the fraternity. Don't pledge Ezra Pound. He's crazy. People been saying that my whole life. So my philosophy is, fuck them. This planet is largely inhabited by imbeciles. I've been in London too long. I've got fog drifting out my ass hole. I'm heading back to Paris. There's just as many damned fools there, but the food's a lot better.

# WASTE LAND

## *Don Nigro*

Seriocomic
Pound, mid thirties

*The poet Ezra Pound has been tirelessly and unselfishly promoting the work of his fellow American expatriate and friend T. S. Eliot, who is still not all that well known. Eliot has just completed the first draft of his long poem, The Waste Land, which, when published, will become one of the seminal works of the twentieth century. But here Eliot, distraught over his disintegrating marriage and very unhappy about his life, has brought his first draft to his friend Ezra for help. Eliot, who protects himself with a mask of rationality, has ripped this revolutionary poem out of the depths of his soul, and at this point has himself believing the poem's no good. He's just been telling that to Pound as Ezra reads it with growing astonishment and wonder. His opening line here is a response to Eliot's suggestion it's a bad poem. Pound is a poet of occasional genius himself, but as he reads, he is realizing that Eliot is a much greater poet. Pound is helping by cutting out parts to make it tighter. As he does so, he sees more and more that he himself will never be this good.)*

### POUND

Mr Eliot, are you out of your fucking mind? Don't you know what you've got here? This is an absolutely original, incredibly brilliant, masterpiece. It's perfect. Absolutely perfect. Except of course you need to take this out.

*(marking something out each time)*

Take this out. This too. And all of this has got to go. And this. And definitely this. Everything here is good. This is not about what's good. This is about what belongs in this particular poem. And this whole section should go. Do not lay so much as one finger on Phlebas, on pain of death. Look. Start with April. End with Shantih. Jesus Christ, this is good. Of course, these lip-diddling chowder-heads are going to be too stupid to see it for a while, but that's always the case. If I ever turn into one of them smug sons of bitches, just take me out and hang me, or put me in the bughouse. You've taken all these fragments and reconstructed a version of Hell as beautiful as Paradise. Of course, Paradise has always only existed in fragments. But you can make excellent sausage out of it. Part of the magic power inherent in fragments is that they're always mysterious. And in that assemblage of broken mirrors you can almost make out the blurred face of the imaginary God. You son of a bitch. You're better than me, you crazy bastard. You just don't know it yet. No, you know it. You're just too polite to say it. Cut this. And this. There. Done.

*(Hands it back to ELIOT.)*

Masterpiece. This and *Ulysses,* and there you have the twentieth century. Jesus Fucking Christ. Where does it come from? What is it? Nobody knows. God, I wish I'd written this fucking thing. What if I just beat out your brains with a chair, dump you in the Thames and put my name on it? Nobody'd ever know the difference.

# WEEDS OF SLOTH

*Mark Bowen*

Comic
Dave, could be any age

*Dave, a waiter, expresses his deep philosophical interpretation of a customer's problems while she waits for her sister to return from the bathroom.*

## DAVE

Well, you see, here's the thing. The way I always seen it, is when somebody don't want you to know something, it usually is for your own good. See, life is like one big Hot Dog Eating contest. Kinda un-American not to like hot dogs. Oh, sorry. You ain't one of them vegetarian gals, are you? Oh boy, thanks be to God there's still some... So, anyways, the rules of that contest: eat as many of them hot dogs and buns as you can in ten minutes, and immediate disqualification for any, uh, "reversal of fortune." You know what that means, don't you? Yeah... you hurl! Oh, sorry I know you and your sister is about to eat. But anyways, you know what they say about hot dogs, the all American food. Food of the gods! But if you ever saw them things getting made, you knew what really went into 'em... you wouldn't never eat 'em, not ever again... Or at the very least you'd have a reversal of fortune before that first one ever touched your lips. So, anyways, you see what I'm sayin'? I'm sure the folks at the weiner companies... they got some files that I ain't never been invited to look into, you know? And you know something? Ignorance is bliss!

For information on this author,
click on the WRITERS tab at www.smithandkraus.com.

# WHAT WE'RE UP AGAINST

## Theresa Rebeck

Dramatic
Stu, thirties-forties

*Stu and another architect at the firm have been trying for months to solve a tricky design problem pertaining to a new mall the firm has been hired to design. A female architect, Eliza, who was hired five months ago and then giving nothing to do has gotten ahold of the plans as they stand and solved the problem, much to the consternation of Stu.*

### STU

It's the system I'm talking about. It's not whether or not she's a woman. It's the fact that she has no respect, this is my point. She comes into my office and says, we need to talk, Stu, and I'm, okay, I'm fine, I can talk, I don't have a problem with this. She has questions. I'm fine with this. She wants to know why I won't let her work. Now, that is not what is happening, I explain that to her. She is a new employee, how long has she been here, five months, six months, this is not–the experience isn't there. That is my point. When the experience is there, she'll be put on projects. She wants to know how she can get the experience if we won't let her work. This is a good question. And so I tell her: Initiative. Initiative, that is how the system works, that is how America works, this is what they don't understand. No one hands you things. You work for them. You earn them. You prove yourself worthy. So she says to me, what about Weber? And I say, what about him? And she says, you let him work. He's been here four months, and you put him on projects. She's jealous. She doesn't care about the work, she just cares, she's competitive, Weber got ahead of her and she doesn't like it. So I say to her, that's got nothing to do with you. This isn't about competition. This is about business. We use the best person for the job. If you prove yourself, through initiative, to be the best person, to be worthy, we will use you. I'll tell you what she said. This, she tells me, she stopped by Weber's office and picked up a copy of that mall extension you guys are working on, the Cambridge Galleria thing. So she's got your design, right? She brings me this design, she tells me she got it from Weber, and then she says, I can see putting Ben on this, he's got seniority. But why does Weber get to work, and not me? What is so good about what he does? She's pissing me off now, because I explained this to her, it's not about competition, I said that, but if she wants to play this game, fine, I'll show her why Weber got the project. So I go through it. Every detail. I show her how every detail indicates that Weber has experience. I prove it to her. And you know what she says to me? "I designed that." She put Weber's name on one of her designs. She came up with her own design for that fucking mall, and then she pretended it was Weber's. She tricked me. This fucking woman stands there–she stands there, and says to me, "This is my point, Stu. It's not about the work, it's about point of view. When a woman designs it, it's shit, and when a man designs it, it's great." So I say to her, no this isn't about point of view, this is about power. You're trying to cut off my balls here. She says, look at the design, Stu, you know it's good, and I say, I don't give a shit if it's good. You want to play by these rules, I can play by these rules. It's shit. Get out of my face. She says, I want to work. Why won't you let me work? And I say fuck you. What you want is power. You come in here and try and cut off my balls, I welcomed you, and this is what you do. This is what we're up against.

For information on this author,
click on the WRITERS tab at www.smithandkraus.com.

# WHAT WE'RE UP AGAINST
## Theresa Rebeck

Dramatic
Weber, forties - fifties

*Weber is the head of a team at an architecture firm which has been trying for month to solve a thorny problem pertaining to a mall design the team is working on. Here, he pontificates to his team on the metaphor of the mall.*

### WEBER

Where there is no history, we create history because history is a construct in which commerce can take place. Commerce. Malls. Malls. History! And that doesn't mean, okay, there's no question people can live without context. People do it all the time. You look at the strip malls of LA, the giant box culture of the midwest, those places survive and even thrive at times, with no gesture whatsoever to the more inchoate yearnings toward time and space and meaning. The human heart meets the void in those places and shops anyway, you don't have to make it a meaningful event beyond you know, what it is. Shopping. But you can't, there's a cultural question which rises out of that that that * aesthetic degradation which posits that nihilistic shopping is what we want, is what we are. We can tolerate it, yes; as a species we can tolerate shopping in just like a giant—. But the three of us are here in this room because somebody somewhere believes we can do better. If strip malls were all we needed, really? That would be all that's out there. And it's not. I mean, even the Mall of America, which is an enormous testament to the conviction that buying and selling is what matters, not the thing bought or sold, and that what is relevant is just the pilgrimage to the place, to the temple of mammon, people coming just to worship the act of shopping—even there, there is history. Seriously, we should get a copy of their layout, it's absolutely mind-blowing, what they put together out there. And how brilliant that it's in Minnesota! The heartland. It redefines from the center the meaning of America. The bonfire, the town green, the shopping mall, the place where people meet to share a meal, where teenagers come to flirt and fall in love, where children run and old people take their walks. This is more than space and time but space and time give context, you know, and everything that belongs in this space and time needs to be held there by history. Because history may be a fiction, but it's a sustainable fiction.

For information on this author,
click on the WRITERS tab at www.smithandkraus.com.

# YEAR'S END
## Joseph Krawczyk

Dramatic
Jack, early forties

*Jack, a high school teacher, tells his colleagues about his intimate relationship with a female student.*

### JACK

You've got to understand ...I have to live with what I've done for the rest of my life. I needed someone with a great heart. Someone who knew how I felt. I don't know why, but I could talk to her for hours. A seventeen-year-old girl. And in those hours I forgot how young she was, because she listened without saying a word. I wasn't afraid to open up for the first time in my life. And she listened to my every fear, and she was sympathetic. I held out my hand, and she touched me. Like no one else had ever done before. She put half of my life back together. God knows I should have left her alone, to find someone else to help me out, but how could I? Ever since I enrolled in the seminary my life was outlined for me. As I approached middle age, I realized what I was in for. And when I worked up enough courage to leave, I had nowhere to go, so I became a high school teacher. I exchanged one set of walls for another. For as long as I can remember, I always wanted to be a writer, and I swore that when I left the church I would experience everything imaginable. But I couldn't bring myself to get close to anyone, really close. I didn't know how. And I couldn't compose a single, worthwhile line. She saw what I couldn't see, what I wanted to see. She was a poet in spite of her father. God bless her....Don't look at me like that, because I'm not a monster. She had a choice, too. Besides, the Sandra we know doesn't really exist. To me, she was a muse. To you, she's the ideal girl you never had. To Mike, a friend who saw him for what he really is. But she's just a kid, smarter, more talented, but mixed up like the rest of us.

For information on this author,
click on the WRITERS tab at www.smithandkraus.com.

# RIGHTS & PERMISSIONS

ALIVE AND WELL © 2016 by Kenny Finkle. Reprinted by permission Beth Blickers, Agency for the Performing Arts. For performance rights, contact Broadway Play Publishing, 212-772-8334, www.broadwayplaypubl.com.

ALLIGATOR © 2016 by Hilary Bettis. Reprinted by permission of Ally Shuster, Creative Artists. For performance rights, contact Ally Shuster (ally.shuster@caa.com)

AMAZING © 2016 by Brooke Berman. Reprinted by permission of Brooke Berman. For performance rights, contact Broadway Play Publishing, 212-772-8334, www.broadwayplaypubl.com.

THE ARSONISTS © 2016 by Jacqueline Goldfinger. Reprinted by permission of Amy Wagner, Abrams Artists Agency. For performance rights, contact Amy Wagner (amy.wagner@abramsartny.com).

BARBECUE APOCALYPSE © 2016 by Matt Lyle. Reprinted by permission of Matt Lyle. For performance rights, contact Broadway Play Publishing, 212-772-8334, www.broadwayplaypubl.com.

BAR BY THE F © 2001 by Sheila Callaghan. Reprinted by permission of Chris Till, Creative Artisrs Agency. For performance rights, contact Chris Till (ctill@caa.com).

THE BELLE OF BELMAR © 2016 by Nicole Pandolfo. Reprinted by permission of Nicole Pandolfo. For performance rights, contact Nicole Pandolfo (nicole.e.pandolfo@gmail.com).

BIG CITY © 2016 by Barbara Blumenthal-Ehrlich. Reprinted by permission of Barbara Blumenthal-Ehrlich. For performance rights, contact Barbara Blumenthal-Ehrlich (barbaretc@aol.com).

BIG SKY © 2016 by Alexandra Gersten-Vassilaros. Reprinted by permission of ICM Partners. For performance rights, contact Ross Weiner, ICM Partners (rweiner@icmpartners.com.)

BIRDS OF A FEATHER © 2016 by June Guralnik. Reprinted by permission of June Guralnik. For performance rights, contact June Guralnik (june@juneguralnick.com).

BREATHING TIME © 2009 by Beau Willimon. Reprinted by permission of Chris Till, Creative Artists Agency. For performance rights, contact Dramatists Play Service, 440 Park Ave. S., New York, NY 10016 (www.dramatists.com) (212-683-8960).

HOUSE RULES © 2014 by A. Rey Pamatmat. Reprinted by permission of Beth Blickers Agency for the Performing Arts. For performance rights, contact Beth Blickers (bblickers@apa-agency.com).

THE JAG © 2016 by Gino DiIorio. Reprinted by permission of Gino DiIorio. For performance rights, contact Elaine Devlin, Elaine Devlin Literary (edevlinlit@aol.com).

KENTUCKY © 2016 by Leah Nanako Winkler. Reprinted by permission of Beth Blickers, Agency for the Performing Arts. For performance rights, contact Beth Blickers (bblickers@apa-agency.com).

THE KID CULT COSMOLOGY © 2016 by Graham Techler. Reprinted by permission of Graham Techler. For performance rights, contact Graham Techler (graham.techler@gmail.com).

KILLING WOMEN © 2014 by Marisa Wegrzyn. Reprinted by permission of Chris Till, Creative Artists Agency. For performance rights, contact Broadway Play Publishing, 212-772-8334, www.broadwayplaypubl.com.

LADIES DAY © 2016 by Alana Valentine. Reprinted by permission of Peregrine Whittlesey, Peregrine Whittlesey Agency. For performance rights, contact Peregrine Whittlesey (pwwagy@aol.com).

THE LEGEND OF GEORGIA MCBRIDE © 2016 by Matthew Lopez. Reprinted by permission of Kevin Lin, Creative Artists Agency. For performance rights, contact Dramatists Play Service, 440 Park Ave. S., New York, NY 10016 (www.dramatists.com) (212-683-8960).

LIFE SUCKS © 2016 by Aaron Posner. Reprinted by permission of Aaron Posner. For performance rights, contact Dramatists Play Service, 440 Park Ave. S., New York, NY 10016 (www.dramatists.com) (212-683-8960).

LOST IN LIMBO © 2016 by Nicholas Priore. Reprinted by permission of Nicholas Priore. For performance rights, contact Nicholas Priore (brokenrecord6@gmail.com).

LULLABY © 2016 by Michael Elyanow. Reprinted by permission of Beth Blickers, Agency for the Performing Arts. For performance rights, contact Beth Blickers (bblickers@apa-agency.com).

MAGIC TRICK © 2016 by Mariah McCarthy. Reprinted by permission of Mariah McCarthy. For performance rights, contact Mariah McCarthy (mariahmwrites@gmail.com).

A MOON FOR THE MISGOTTEN AT THE CHARLESVILLE SUMMER THEATRE FESTIVAL © 2016 by Graham Techler. Reprinted by permission of Graham Techler. For performance rights, contact Graham Techler (graham.techler@gmail.com).